The Horse Watcher

Answers to Questions
You never knew you had

Linda Finstad

ISBN:10:150:5548535
ISBN:13:978-1505548532

Foreword

Since ancient times the behavior of wild horses has fascinated horse lovers both young and old, myself included.

Many studies have been done to better understand how these wild horses communicate, survive, and thrive without any help from man. However,truly wild horses make up a very small percentage of the Worlds Equine population. The vast majority of horses are born and raised in captivity (domestic animals).
Which begs the question:
Has man's influence changed their natural way of being – do they still speak the same language as their wild counterparts?
Have domestic horses been robbed of their natural instincts, and trained to behave in a way that is more pleasing to man?

The key to unlocking this mystery was to "Un-Think" what I thought I knew and be totally objective in my observations and conclusions.
I spent countless hours watching, photographing and documenting herds of horses both wild and domestic. My goal was to try and think like a horse in an attempt to understand why they do what they do. Some of theses sessions posed more questions than answers, with more investigation required. In some cases, experiments were designed to help uncover the truth.

The answers and insights this study revealed will surprise even the most seasoned horsemen and women.
In an attempt to "show and tell" this book is laid out in an easy to follow question and answer format along with some beautiful photographs. You can start at the beginning or the end or anywhere in between.
Each page is filled with fascinating information.

Kudos

This project would not have been possible without the cooperation, help and enthusiasm of a large number of horse owners and breeders. All of them welcomed me into their fields to observe and study their horses.
I feel honored to have worked with them and value their insights and friendship, This book is dedicated to them.

Also to my family who supported my dream - they patiently listened as I raved about the exploits of various horses. Became self sufficient when I disappeared on field research for weeks on end, they even helped to build props for the experiments, even when they secretly thought they were crazy.
Also a big Thank You to all the horse owners who participated in the experiments.

Linda Finstad
The Horse Watcher

Answers to Questions

Topics

It all starts with a foal

Wouldn't it be great if you knew exactly what horses were thinking?
If we were in tune with the needs and objectives of each othe,
There would be a lot less frustration from both sides.
Well the good news is – Horses are a lot less complicated than people.
It is easier to study the natural behavior and communication of horses both wild and domestic than it is to understand how the average teenagers mind works.
My name is Linda Finstad – I am "Horse Watcher".
My goal is to inspire you to become a horse watcher, too.
It is easy to do, and requires no previous experience or special equipment.
I must warn you, once you wander down this path of enlightenment there is no going back – the truth will set you free.
OK that was a little dramatic, but I do want you to approach the insights and information I am about to share with an open and inquiring mind.
If we are to "Think like a Horse" in an attempt to understand why horses do what they do,

We need to start at the very beginning.

With the Development of a Foal (embryo)

Once fertilization has taken place the remarkable process of cell division begins. In only 21 days it goes from a microscopic
single cell - to a tiny embryo the size of a pea.

This might not seem very big, but a heartbeat can already be detected

At around 60 days, with the aid of an ultrasound, the sex of the foal can be determined. The embryo is now the size of a hamster.

During the first 6 months of pregnancy, a lot is happening
Organs are being formed - limbs and bone develop
The fetus is now the size of an average house cat.

It is during the last few months that the fetus grows rapidly.
He goes from the size of a cat to a perfectly formed foal weighing around 100 - 125lbs, depending on the breed.

How many foals can a mare produce?

A healthy, well- managed mare can produce a foal every year into her twenties.
She is sexually mature at age 3
So could possibly produce as many as 17 foals. Most breeders and owners wouldn't push a mare to produce that many.

How Long is a mares Pregnancy?

The general rule is 340 days
but some mares will go well over that.

In the wild, a mare chooses the cover of darkness to give birth, as she considers this to be the safest time of day.
She won't be bothered by other horses, and the herd is less likely to be on the move at night.
The threat of preditors who might see her baby as an easy meal is also less of a worry.
Interestingly - domestic horses also prefer to give birth at night.

Do horses need help foaling?

In the wild, the mare will foal alone. If there are any complications nature will decide their fate.
This is unlike domesticated horses, where the mare is kept in a large foaling stable with lots of deep warm straw prior to her delivery. Some owners set up baby   moniters in the stable so they can watch her progress but still allow her peace and quiet. As soon as it starts, they are there to lend a hand and make sure the foal is OK - they may either have a vet on hand or have him on speed dial.

Do horses have twins?

Horses are not designed to carry and nourish two fetuses. Double pregnancies put both mare and foal at risk.

If a mare does concieve twins, very often her body will naturally abort either one or both of the foals.

Occasinally twins are carried to term and born healthy.

Twins are more common in donkeys than horses, but carry the same risk.

Will equine twins be identical?

Twins occur when the mare ovulates an egg from each of her two ovarian follicles and both eggs are fertilized, resulting in two embryos.

It is extremely rare that a fertilized egg splits to form identical twins.

Did you know?

Foals are born with legs that are 90% of their full adult length.

They are able to stand very soon after they are born.

In the wild, it is very important for mother and baby to move away from the birth site as soon as possible, because the smell of fluids and afterbirth will quickly attract predators.

Foal fatality

The loss of a foal during pregnancy or soon after birth is always sad. According to researchers "placenitis" is the most common cause of foal fatality. This is inflamation of the placenta the temporary organ that forms to support the foal while inside the mare during pregnancy.

Placentitis may cause the horse to abort the foal before its time. If the mare goes full term her foal may be very weak or even still born.

Immediately after being born, a foal can see, hear, and smell almost as well as a mature horse.

The newborn foal will have no teeth, but within the first week of life he will develop four incisors, two in the upper jaw and two in the lower jaw.
By 6 months of age, he will have a full set of 24 baby teeth.
These will eventually be pushed out by his permanent teeth.
He will have his full set of between 36 - 44 permanent teeth by the time he is 5 years old.

What is colostrum?

The first milk a foal gets from its mother is "colostrum". This milk is very important and can mean the difference between life and death.
The mare only produces this thick yellow "foal's first food" for 24 hours after giving birth.
The foal's immune system needs colostrum to function. Without it, he has no defences to fight off infection. This vitaly important colostrum will keep him healthy until his own immune system is functioning properly at about 8 - 10 weeks of age.
Once the colostrum is all gone, the mare produces milk to nourish her foal.

How long will a foal suckle?

The simple answer is;
As long as the mare will allow.

Foals will start to nibble grass when they are just a few days old.
But they will get most of their nutrition from their mothers milk.
For the first 6 - 8 weeks of life. foals need this protein rich milk.

After that they will graze more and more.

9

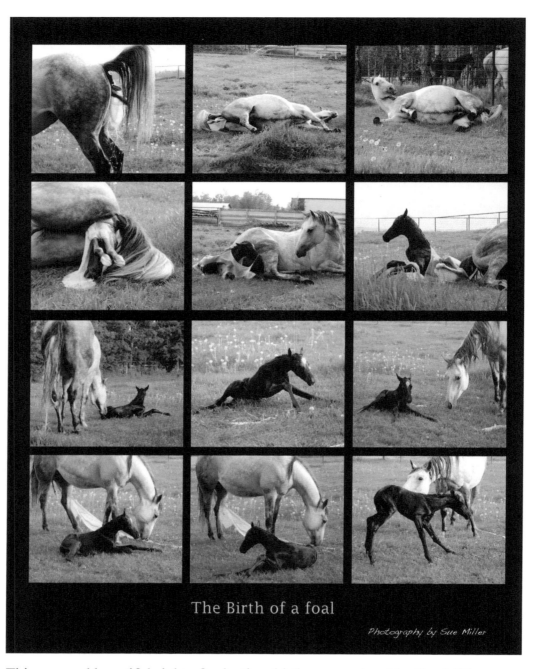

The Birth of a foal

Photography by Sue Miller

This rare and beautiful sight of a daytime birth was captured by Sue Miller, allowing us to clearly see the various stages of birth.

This little colt was eager to test his legs just a few moments after his arrival into the world.

Horses cant talk so
How do we know when a mare is ready to give birth?

She will "Bag up".
During the last month the mare's udder will enlarge, and fill with milk. It will fill up overnight while the mare is resting, and shrink during the day as she moves around. This is the first sign that the mare is nearing her time.

Her pelvic area will start to change shape.
These changes allow the fetus to pass through the birth canal with greater ease. A "hollow" develops around either side of the root of the tail as the muscles around the hip and buttocks start to relax.

Waxing
The last sign is waxing - these are wax-like beads that appear on the teats, they are in fact small beads of Colostrum. It would be nice if this happened consistently with all mares, but some will wax up a week before giving birth, others within 12 - 24 hours, while some don't wax up at all.

Relaxation of the Vulva
The vulva will become swollen and elongated, usually in the last 24 - 48 hours before the birth
During the birth, it will stretch several times its normal size to allow for the passage of the foal.

Sweaty and restless
As the mare nears the delivery time, she may be feeling some discomfort and pain; she might kick at her abdomen, swish her tail, and continually look at her tail. These are similar signs to that of colic.
As labor starts she will break out into a sweat

When the waters break - showtime
The placental sac breaks, releasing a gush of amniotic fluid (breaking water). This fluid lubricates the birth canal and the foal.
The mare will lie down on her side and start to push. Horses experience powerful contractions and will often groan and grunt as they push the foal out.
As the mare pushes, you will see the foals front legs start to protrude, covered in a white shiny sac. The nose and head should appear once the front legs are out to about the knees.
The foal's rear feet will often remain in the birth canal as the mare and newborn take a rest.
The umbilical cord is still attached and transferring large, vital amounts of blood from mare to foal.
This 5 - 15 minute rest is crucial and the mare should not be rushed.
After her rest period, the mare will stand and break the umbilical cord

Usually the foal should stand and begin to nurse within 2 - 6 hours after birth.

"You never get a second chance to make a good first impression"

This popular quote we have all heard
is also true in nature.

When a foal is first born, his mother will vigorously lick and nudge her foal to stimulate his circulation and encourage him to stand.

She uses touch - sight - smell and sound to create a bond. It is very important that the mare and foal not only bond, but are able to recognise each other's sound and smell, especially in the wild or in a large domestic herd.

In those first few days, the mare will keep her foal away from other horses. Not because she is worried they will harm or attack her baby, but she doesn't want her baby to imprint on another horse. If this new baby tried to suckle from the

wrong mare, he would be rejected and go hungry or worse, kicked and injured.

What a foal learns in those first few hours and days will stay with him all his life.

Why do some foals form strong bonds with humans?

Some breeders are using this natural learning mechanism to imprint themselves onto the foal.

Imprinting is very "Trendy". There are numerous books on this subject. However it is a controversial topic.
Some breeders are very much in favor of this early training method, but many are adamantly opposed.

The process begins in the first hour of the foal's life, with the handler toweling the foal dry. Replacing the mares touch and smell with his own, he gently talks to the foal, allowing the foal to learn the sound of his voice.
This starts the de-sensatization process. The handler will continue to run his hands all over the foal's body.

Over the course of 30 days, the foal is repeatedly handled and introduced to new things - like having his feet picked out, being groomed and wearing a halter.
The foal will also be introduced to typically "spooky" things like plastic bags, newspaper, aerosol spray, clippers etc.

The results of imprinting and early training are permanent; the foal will grow into a horse which is unafraid, but respectful of humans.

Many mares do not take kindly to this invasion of their personal space. The handler is preventing her from doing her job as a mother.

The way to a foal's heart is through his mother

There is research to support that positive handling and grooming of the mare in the first few days after birth also affects the way the foal responds to humans. Horses learn by example and "if Mom is happy to be handled, there isn't be anything to be scared of".

Are all foals born equal?

When a foal is born into a herd, he adopts his mom's place in the herd and all the privileges that may or may not go with that place. For example a foal of the alpha mare will by default become the alpha foal and enjoy first choice of grazing and first drink at the watering hole at the side of his mother.

The same is true of the foal born to the last place mare - her foal will be the lowest of the low in the herd.

However this status only lasts while the foal is nursing. Once weaned, he will have to establish his own place in the hierarchy.

When should you wean a foal?

Weaning is potentially one of the most stressful experiences in a young horses life. Although foals can be weaned at 4 months because by this age they need more nutrition than can be supplied by mother's milk; generally they are left with their mothers longer.

In the wild, weaning is very gradual, and the youngster will stay with his Mother until she has another foal. Then he will join the other yearlings in the herd.

What is polite behavior?

When a foal is born, his "ego" has not yet been developed. He is polite and listens to his instincts to stay out of trouble and keep him safe and likable in the herd.

He does not want to make trouble or draw attention to himself.

The way he operates is to move away from anything that moves towards him and follow anything that is leaving.

These two responses carry a lot of social protection and politeness.

Keeping juvenile horses with only their peers, as often happens, promotes unruly behavior.

Researchers reached this conclusion after comparing the behavior of immature horses before and after adult horses joined the group.

When two mares were added to a group of fillies, or two geldings to a group of colts, the young horses' social skills improved substantially.

With the adults' influence, the one and two-year-olds became less aggressive, resorting less often to biting and kicking.

At the same time, the young horses grew more sociable, and more frequently displayed positive social interaction.

The youngsters learned new behaviors after the adults were introduced, which seemed to influence which herd mates they associated with.

Mature horses have a positive influence on how yearlings and two-year-old horses behave.

The same applies in the wild

Observations of wild horses find that when greater numbers of adults are around, yearlings and two-year-olds act less aggressively. Youngsters are chastised by both male and female herd members. The punishment to a young animal is swift, usually just a head movement with ears laid back or a nip or gentle kick. It is clear both domestic and wild horses behave better with adult supervision.

It takes a village (herd) to raise a foal

Foals enjoy hanging out together, they play, form friendships, groom each other and establish a hierarchy within their peer group - very similar to kindergarten.
Although they think they are stepping out on their own, the rest of the herd is quietly baby sitting.
Everyone watches out for, and feels responsible for the youngest members of their family (herd).
This includes occasionally chastising them if they are rude or disrespectful.

The mares quietly stand and babysit whilst the foals rest

What is "snapping" foal behavior?

Snapping is a submissive behavior in which the foal opens and closes his mouth, rhythmically snapping his teeth together.
It looks like the foal is talking but no sound is coming out.
They will do this to everyone and everything, mares, stallions, and humans even trees and unusual objects.

It is an appeasement gesture
"Please don't hurt me, I am just a baby"

What causes some mares to be "moody" ?

Moody behavior is often associated with the mares oestrous cycle.
The ovarian hormones can have a significant impact on a mares mood, level of arousal, sensitivity to pain and patience.
Her levels of oestrogen and progesterone go up and down as the mare goes through her normal oestrous cycle.
Behaviors such as tail swishing, kicking, squealing, and reluctance to work are all normal.

But what about when things go wrong!

Just imagine your prized mare has just given birth to her first, long-awaited foal. The new filly appears healthy and strong and quickly begins her attempts to stand. After several spectacular crashes, she finally makes it to her feet.
Your mare suddenly becomes anxious, then obviously distressed. She lunges at the foal, ears pinned, teeth bared...

She is rejecting the foal.
Fortunately the above scenario is not a common one, but foal rejection definitely occurs and is a serious problem when it does

Why do some mares reject their foals?
Rejection is most common amongst first time mothers. The mare may find the whole process overwhelming and scary.
A painful birth resulting in stress and anxiety may be the cause.
Too many people present at the birth or if she foals in a herd setting with too many other mares around could also be the cause.

Foal rejection can be divided into three categories:

Avoidance: This usually seems to be a fear-based reaction.
The mare will run away from the approaching foal. She will not intentionally hurt the foal; however, if the mare and foal are confined to a small area, such as a small box stall, the mare might accidentally run over or step on the foal.

Not allowing foal to nurse: This is the most common maternal behavior problem, again occuring with first-time mothers. Udder problems such as mastitis or a painful, swollen udder may be to blame.
Other times, the mare will allow humans to milk her, but will not allow the foal to nurse, which means it is just the foal's nursing to which she objects and not a purely pain-based reaction.

Aggression by the mare toward the foal.
Although aggression is the least common, it is the most serious. The mare deliberately attacks, kicking, or biting the foal over the neck and back.

Most aggressive mares will not attack their foals while they are lying down. The cause of this unprovoked aggression is unknown. The attacks usually come when the foal is standing or when the foal nears the mare's food.

When agression occurs, the owners would separate the mare and foal and if possible find a foster mare for the foal. If one was not available the foal would be bottle fed and classed as an orphan foal.

Orphan foals are high maintenance; they require feeding every two hours for the first few days.

Which also begs the question;

How much milk should an orphan foal drink?

At one day of age, his intake should be equal to 10% of his body weight;

Bt 10 days of age,that figure should be gradually increased to 25% of his body weight, until he is weaned.

For example, a 100-pound foal could consume 25 pounds of milk a day, or 50 cups.

Owners ensure there is the correct balance of nutrients and the foal is closely monitored for growth, food consumption, and weight gain.

With lots of TLC, they can grow to be every bit as tall, strong, and athletic as foals raised by their dams.

In the wild
An orphan foal would not share the same good fortune.

What is pasture breeding?

Pasture breeding happens when a stallion is turned out with a group of mares.
This method mimics the natural family unit found in the wild.
Stallions are allowed to court the mares when they come into season and breed
without human intervention. Just as nature intended
The situation seems idyllic.

Courtship: The stallion politely approaches the mare
Only if the mare is receptive and ready will mating take
place.

Do Stallions attack foals?

Mares and foals can usually be pasture bred safely.

Most stallions will not bother a mare's foal. It is important that there is plenty of room so the foals can escape any aggresive behavior.

What is Hand Breeding

Hand breeding is probably the most widely used method of breeding horses. Usually one person handles or holds the mare to be bred while another person handles the stallion.

The stallion is brought to the mare and allowed to mount and breed the mare naturally.

The mare should have been teased previously and known to be in heat. Very often the mare's hind legs will be hobbled in some manner so she cannot kick the stallion and stallion handlers.

The mare will have had her tail wrapped and her external genitalia cleaned.

This process is efficient and hygenic, but not terribly romantic.

What is Corral Mating?

Another method used to breed horses is referred to as corral mating.

The mare to be bred is turned into a small paddock or "corral" when she is ready to be bred. The stallion is then turned in with the mare. The mare and stallion are then taken out after they have successfully mated. This procedure is used more commonly with young, inexperienced stallions who aren't quite sure of their roles. An older more experienced mare will quickly teach a young stud how he must behave.

How to think like a Horse
Herd Dynamics

The best way to understand how horses behave and communicate is to spend some time sitting in a field with a herd of horses watching the "Herd Dynamics".

 Horses are intuitively dependant on other herd members for their survival; there is safety in numbers. It's important that each horse that makes up the herd learns how to fit in and get along with everyone else.

In the wild, to be banished from the herd is like a death sentance.

So, it is easy to see why herd rules and hierarchy exist in wild horses; but after thousands of years of domestication, with humans looking after the horses' needs you might think that "herd mentality" would have faded from view, if not completely been bred out of our domestic horses.

Not True

The Herd instinct and need for understanding one's place in the herd is still very evident and functioning perfectly.

If you spend some time observing horses in their field it will soon become apparent who is the alpha female and also who is lowest horse in the pecking order.

Alpha female – Matriarch – Lead horse

All names given to the most prominent mare in the herd.

The alpha female is usually a mature, stronger mare (not necessarily the biggest) she is streetwise, she decides when the herd should move to new pasture, and when to go and drink from the water hole. She commands so much respect from the other herd members; that if a horse is acting disrespectfully or pushing its boundaries, all it takes is a "look" from her and the other horse will back away. She very rarely needs to resort to flamboyant signs of aggression such as biting or kicking. She keeps everyone in check, as her title suggests.

However there is no particular benefit to holding this position as it carries its own set of responsibilities and very few perks. Her reward for this responsibility is commanding a larger personal space and being able to pick the best patch of grass on which to graze.

This system works perfectly, which is why for the most part horses look calm and peaceful when you see them grazing in a field.

The position no horse wants to hold is last place in the herd. In the wild the last place horse is usually old, sick or lame and typically the one predaors will go after.

In a domestic herd last place might be the youngest or newest horse to be introduced to the herd.

The Loner (lowest horse in the pecking order)

This horse has the lowest social standing and is pushed to the back at feeding time.

He may be the horse who always seems to be alone - kind of apart from the rest of the horses. This behavior may be mistaken as aloofness or "liking their own space" but being apart from the main group is not a personal choice. The horse would be much happier hanging out with the rest of the horses if they would let him.

It is better to be in the middle of the pack quietly minding your own business and staying out of trouble.

Fights between middle and high-ranking horses rarely break out. Squabbles are more likely between the bottom placed horses, and happens mostly when new horses are introduced to the herd.

They see this as their opportunity to move up the ladder in the herd.

Why are some horses bullies?

Sometimes this kind of behavior appears for no apparent reason. A horse may chase or bite another horse in the field or launch a full on attack if he gets too close. Contrary to popular belief, bullying is not usually done by the Alpha horse.

Horses will test each other all the time - horses who are insecure in their standing in the herd may "bully" the ones under them, just because he can

Only in captivity are horses "forced" into un-natural Herds

I want you to think about that for a moment

In the wild horses live in family groups - a dominant stallion and his mares and young-stock. Chances are, all these horses will be related.

Bachelor groups of young males form out of a need for companionship and safety - it is in their best interest to band together, as lone horses are an easy target for predators. The bachelors may or may not be related.

21

Why do horses breathe into each other's nostrils?

When horses meet for the first time - or after separation, they will exchange exhalations through their nostrils.

This is how they say Hello! they do recall each others' breaths, just like we remember the names of people we meet.

After a few initial breaths, the intensity of "huffing" will increase or decrease depending on the information exchanged.

Increased harder breathing can be a sign of one horse exerting dominance and can lead to biting - squealing - striking out or turning around to pummel the other horse with kicks from his hind legs.

It is best to keep a safe distance during those first meeting exchanges.

Do Horses have a BFF?

YES - absolutely some horses (not all) form a very special friendship with another horse and they become pair-bonded. They want to do everything together, eat, sleep even roll at the same time, and they refuse to be separated.

This can be a problem for their owners.

Why do horses "nibble" each other?

Horses use nipping as a form of Communication. Did you ever watch a horse who had an itch? He will walk over to another herd mate and start to nibble the second horse in the same spot that itches on his own body. The second horse will start nibbling the itchy spot on the first horse. As the first itch gets cared for, the first horse will move its nibbling to another spot, and the second horse will be nibbling the new spot... And so on
The communication is very clear, they are happy to help each other out.

22

Why do horses sleep standing up?

It is a survival need. In the wild, when startled or alarmed by predators, the horse will survive by his fight or flight response. If you have ever watched a horse get up from a lying down position you will have noticed how slow and awkward it seems. This delay could mean the difference between life and death.

How do they do that - without falling over?

Horses have something called "stay apparatus" which is a unique adaptation of the musclosketal system. It allows the horse to lock limbs in position so that very little muscle function is required.

In the front legs, the stay apparatus is always in place so the horse only needs to relax to take advantage of it.

However to use the stay apparatus in the hind leg, a horse must rotate his hip and literally hook one bone up over

Do horses Snore?

Just like humans, some do and some don't.
but you only have to walk into the barn late at night to hear it for yourself!

How much sleep does a horse need?

Around 3 hours in a 24 hour period They will doze whilst standing up but they also need deep REM (rapid eye movement) sleep to be fully rested. They need to be lying down to achieve REM sleep, but they only need 15 mins of REM per day. Foals sleep more than adult horses. They spend half their day napping.

---

a knob on another bone. The stifle and hock lock into a fixed position bearing all the weight of the horse's hind end. The other leg is usually in a flexed relaxed position.

23

Why do horses roll?

You only have to watch a horse roll to realize he is doing it because it's fun and feels good.

But why just after a bath?

One theory is that as the hair on his back dries it gets tight and itchy; to get down and roll is the perfect way to ditch the itch.

Doesn't he like being clean?

Horses like to find mud to roll in, as this coating of mud and dust gives them some protection from the attacks of biting insects.

How do I know when a horse is going to roll?

He will exhibit one or more of the following actions: pacing in a circle, pawing the ground, blowing the dirt with his nostrils, slightly bending his knees and leaning to one side. If you are mounted, this would be a good time to get off and remove the saddle.

Is Rolling good for horses?

Yes - The way a horse rolls is an indicator of his health. A healthy horse with a good strong back will roll vigorously from one side to the other without standing up. Horses with high withers may roll on one side get up and lay down immediately to roll on the other side. This is nothing to worry about; its just that his conformation won't allow him to roll completely over.

An unhealthy horse or one with a weak back may roll on one side very briefly get up and walk away. Some horses will refuse to roll at all.

Rolling plays a very important part in a horse's health. When he rolls, he is stretching all the muscles in his spine, neck, barrel, flanks and buttocks.

24

How do horses show affection to each other?

Nickering - a soft sound they make to greet one another

Scratching - Horses often use their teeth to scratch the itch of a friend - the friend will return the gesture.

Mutual grooming - Like scratching, mutual grooming is another way horses can touch each other to show affection. They may stand nose to tail using their tails to flick flies away from a friend's face. They use their teeth to rub burrs, seeds and debris from another's mane.

Head resting or hugging - horses hug one another by resting their head and necks over that of a friend - this indicates affection - very often they will doze this way.

Nuzzling - mares and foals are always nuzzling each other. The babies will also rub up against their mom's.

Horses are extremly affectionate. You only have to take the time to watch them in the field "just being horses" to see all these displays of affection.

Do horses gasp for breath?

No - Horses can't breathe through their mouths.
They only breath through their noses.

Why do horses kick and bite?

You may be just too close for comfort!

"It is said that a horse is dangerous at both ends and crafty in the middle"
There are many possible reasons that a horse will strike out. One is that his personal space has been invaded, and it is a warning for the intruder "back off". That personal space varies greatly with different individuals, circumstances, and experiences. Some horses react violently when their space is invaded.

It is believed that when a horse reaches out and gently touches you, he is giving you permission to touch him.

Can horses wink?

This is kind of a trick question - horses do not wink in the same way humans do.

Winking is a term used to describe a behavior a mare displays when she comes into her heat cycle, to let the stallion know she is ready to breed. Winking is when the mare opens and closes the lower part of her vulva.

Do horses recognize their family members?

There is no science to prove or test this. However, based on my field research and observations, I think they do.

Horses have excellent memories, so if they have met and exchanged breaths, they will remember each other.

Do horses speak?

Although horses mainly communicate through body language, they also have a varied vocal repetoire:

Nickering

Whinnying

Neighing

Squealing

Snorting and Blowing

So what is the difference between these sounds and

Why do Horses do that?

The Snort When a horse snorts, he's normally very alert because snorting is often used to communicate possible danger to his herd mates.
The horse usually holds his head high while exhaling through the nose with his mouth shut. The strong exhale creates a vibration or flutter sound in the nostrils. The snort lasts about one second and can be heard up to 30 feet away.
He will plant his feet and stare intensely at the object he's unsure about. Horses will snort when they hear something unusual, smell strange smalls, or see something they don't expect. Horses may also snort when they come into contact with a new horse or one that they feel threatened by.

The Blow - much like the snort. The horse exhales through his nose with his mouth shut. The blow does not create the vibrating or fluttering noise that the snort does. It is usually used when a horse is curious, or when the horse meets another. The strength of the blow and body movements that follow will tell you what the horse is saying.

The Nicker - from his vocal cords the horse creates a soft vibrating sound with his mouth closed. The strength and tone of the nicker vary greatly, and will tell you what the horse is saying. it is generally used as a friendly greeting.

Stallions will nicker to potential mates to get their attention.

A mare will nicker quietly to her foal to encourage him to come closer. The mare may also nudge her foal towards her flanks to protect him from danger.

The Neigh is the loudest and longest of the horse sounds. The neigh is not a sound of fear. It is used when a horse is being separated from others.

"Is anyone else here?" - The horse neighs with his head high, looking around for other horses or people. The horse usually neighs several times (if the horse neighs after a companion has answered his neigh, he is usually saying "Where are you".

The Squeal A horse squeals with his mouth closed. The squeal can be short and quiet or loud and long. The squeal can be heard far away if the horse squeals loud enough.

A horse may squeal while backing off, or sometimes aggressively approaching the object that is pushing or upseting him.

The Scream is an expression of aggression and sounds like a loud roar. It is only used during a fight between two horses, usually only in the wild.

Did you know?

The horse's teeth can pick up vibrations transmitted through the ground as he grazes - these vibrations are conveyed to the middle ear through the jawbone.

He can also pick up low frequency vibrations through his hooves which alerts him to predators.

It is extremely hard to sneak up on a horse, which is why they have survived for thousands of years.

What are the roles and responsibilities of the stallion?

I have had the great fortune to be witness to both wild horses and domestic herds. To be honest, there is very little difference in the stallions behavior. Whilst watching the family group (mares / youngstock and one dominant stallion) the stallion is very easy to spot, as he is the one who seems to be continually "busy".

The mares and foals will gently graze, wander around the pasture and snooze. Foals may frolic and play with each other and engage in social grooming. However, the stallion is hard wired to be on patrol. His job is to look out for possible danger - this may be in the form of a predator or another intruding stallion. The threat to his herd may be real or imaginary, so he will move around the outside of the herd - sniffing at poop to check who is in the herd.

Why does he sniff poop?
Each horse has a unique smell. The stallion will be able to identify each horse in the pasture by its poop.
If he smells something special, or perhaps recognizes that one of the mares is in season by the distinct odor of her poop, he may put his noses in the air and pull his upper lip up. This is called Fleming.

What is a stud pile?
The stallion will gain some comfort in knowing who is in the pasture, but he also will use his own poop to mark his territory and send a signal to other stallions that he is the head of this herd and to back off.
Both wild and domestic stallions create a "Stud pile". This is a place where they repeatedly poop - to mark their territory and let others know who is top horse around here.

I feel it is worth noting that only the stallion will poop on the stud pile - It would be considered extremely rude and totally out of line if another horse in the herd added his scent, and pooped on the stud pile.

I have never personally witnessed this, so, I am not sure what the consequences would be for such a disrespectful act.

If any intruders come into the pasture, he will "move his mares" to a new,   safer location.

28

How does a stallion move his herd ?

All stallions exhibit similar characteristics: they will stretch out their heads and neck so they are long and low and kind of snake their heads from side to side as they encircle the herd, moving them to a new location.

This action may be a gentle suggestion, if the stallion does not feel the threat is too great. Or it can look extremely aggressive - young stallions without the wisdom or experience of older studs tend to react more expressively.

When the herd stallion is agitated or upset, his thoughts are not just for his own safety.

One would think if a horse Sees a cougar or wolf in the bushes, his instinct would be to flee. But the stallion feels responsible for his mares, so his reaction to danger is to move his family to a safer location.

What is also very interesting to watch is the mare's reaction to the stallion.

Pay particular attention to their facial expression and their ears. There is more to this communication behavior than meets the eye.

In every interaction of this kind that I have witnessed the mares all pay attention and comply to the stallion's wishes.

How do horses learn these rules?

Every horse knows more about being a horse than most people know about being human.

Horses teach their young how to behave in a herd (how to stay out of trouble) so a more dominant herd member won't feel the need to chastise them. The education of younger members of the herd seems to be the responsibility of all the herd members both male and female not just the immediate parents.

Horses lead by example it is very much a "Do as I do" system as opposed to the human "Do as I say" system.

We have established that there are rules to maintaining harmony within the herd.

" Snaking"

In the wild, the stallion is constantly on the look out for other young studs who might try and steal his mares or challenge him in a "winner takes all" battle for the right to take over his herd.

This worry is just as real for domestic stallions – even though they have been bred in captivity and understand how metal fences work. They are still agitated and upset by the presence of another stallion, especially if they are running with a herd of mares and young stock.

A stallion's natural instinct is extremely strong.

These two studs are actually friends – although it doesn't look like it from the picture.

During the winter months, they live in adjoining pens - they can sniff and touch each other through the fence and get along really well.

However, all that changes once the older stud is living in the large pasture with "his" mares. Now his winter companion is now a very real threat.

Right off the bat I need to say it really is nothing personal
it is how they are wired.

There is a lot misunderstanding regarding the relationships stallions have with each other.

Stallions don't just hate other stallions. In fact if the group is all male. they can get along perfectly fine together. However, as soon as a mare is introduced into the mix, the dynamics change and it is each guy for himself.

Why do horses wiggle their ears?

If you want a better understanding of how horses communicate, You need to study their ears.

Science has revealed that just like humans, horses read each others' faces. And those expressions go way beyond ears forward " I am happy to see you" or ears pinned back "I am grumpy or mad".

Horses gain lots of important information from each other by watching the ears of the other horses.

Think of the ear movements as "sign language" similar to what deaf people use to communicate - if you know how to sign or have watched others "signing" you know how effective it is.

Some signs are for letters - others indicate emotions or intentions
The actions are fast and quickly understood by someone else who also knows sign language.

Horses have very mobile ears, they can swivel them round almost 180 degrees, point them forward, pull them up, or flatten them back.
Their ears can move independently of each other, so one can point forward and the other backwards.
These ear movements are so important that, if horses' ears are covered up, another horse struggles to know what it is thinking, or trying to communicate.

If you watch the interactions of horses in a pasture, their ears are continually moving - so one can only assume they are using them to not only listen but also communicate many more emotions than just interest or anger.

Why do horses swish their tails?
The obvious answer is to swat flies off their bodies,
however a true horse watcher will look beyond the obvious

The horse's tail is an extension of his spine.
Because of this, you can learn a lot about a horse by watching his tail.
The tail holds clues to his health and emotional state.
Does the horse carry his tail to one side? Does he clamp it down? Or, does he let it hang loosely right down the middle?

Horses who have a lot of tension or pain (especially in their back) will clamp down their tails.
A clamped tail is also an indication that the horses is worried, especially about things coming up from behind.
A horse will often swish its tail slowly back and forth to keep flies off.
But tails are used for more than brushing off flies and insects.

An angry horse will often swish its tail rapidly; this might be a sign that you or something around him irritates him. Treat it as a warning sign especially if he is looking annoyed and pinning his ears. His next move may be to lash out and kick whatever is the source of his irritation.

Excited horses "flag" their tails up, holding it up and away from their bodies. (Some breeds have more extreme tail carriages than others. Arabians are noted for their high tail carriage and often when an Arabian (or part Arabian) gets really excited, the tail will "flop over" onto the horse's back.

Foals also hold their tails high up as they run and play as an expression of joy and excitement.

Mares in heat will carry their tails off to one side as a display to the stallion that they are ready for breeding.

This is all great information but - because it is at the back of the horse it is often overlooked.

The tail or more accurately the dock is an extension of the horse's spine The horse uses his tail for Balance and Impulsion.

As a professional photographer, I spend hours and hours at the rail of both dressage and show jumping arenas – capturing all the action.
 Usually not much attention is paid, to what the horse is doing with his tail.
However, looking back over past show photos, I began to see a pattern.
As they jumped over the higher fences, they did some very interesting things with their tails.
Now you are a "Horse Watcher", I challenge you to pay more attention to ears and tails. Maybe you can unravel the mystery of equine communication.

Why do horses eat thistles even if there is good grass?

The flowering thistle heads are very palatable to horses. The thistle is considered a medicinal herb with liver healing properties Horses generally know what is good for them and will self medicate if those plants and herbs are available to them.

Why do horses eat snow?

If their water source is frozen, a horses will eat snow in the winter to get moisture. However this is a poor substitute for fresh water.

Why do horses sometimes Eat dirt?

Dirt eating or "Geophagia" is seen in both wild and domestic horses. It is believed that a craving for dirt is actually a craving for certain minerals in the dirt, namely iron and copper.

How much food Does a horse need?

A horse will consume around 2% of his total body weight in food to nourish himself and maintain a healthy weight.
He needs to drink 6 - 12 gallons of water per day to stay hydrated.

Just like humans, horses crave different amounts of water.
Their needs will vary depending on the type of food they are eating and work they are doing.

A horse deprived of food but supplied with water can survive 20 - 25 days

A horse deprived of water for just 2 days will stop eating and start exhibiting signs of colic.
Water consumption is extremely important to the horse's digestive process.

Do horses get stressed out?
Horses succumb to many of the same kinds of stresses as humans,
Such as learning new and difficult tasks
Boring, day to day routines and lack of stimulation
Negative reinforcement, bullying or insufficient rewards, troublesome bosses
(In the horse's case trainers)
Lack of other equine company - insufficient fresh air and exercise.
The good news is - when you know the cause you can remove or change it
And relieve stress.

Why do horses Yawn?
Horses do not yawn for the same reasons humans do
It is NOT a sign of boredom.
Horses yawn to relieve stress.If a horse is learning something new in a training
session, he may yawn to release endorphins for a calming effect on the nervous system, once a break is offered. He will typically yawn 3 times
If he is basking in the sun and dozing, he may let go a sleepy yawn
But usually just one.

Why do horses poop on the go?
Partly because they have to.
But also because they are nervous.

When a horse is nervous, it releases adrenaline which in turn rev's up the body for action.
As part of this process the gut gets moving and so does the bowel.

Lighten the load; you might have to run.

What goes in must come out
Did you know
The average horse produces 9 tons of manure every year

An average horse 15:2hh will deposit around 35 pounds of manure daily.

Plus 6 - 10 gallons of urine

Why do Bucking horses BUCK?

Before we can answer that question we must first ask, what makes a bucking horse and how does one end up at the rodeo.

Bred to Buck

The original stock of bucking horses comes from a variety of different backgrounds and includes a good a mixture of different breeds – but they all had one thing in common - they all bucked, which made them undesirable riding horses, but perfect for rodeo. Which is why you will see many different colors and types at the rodeo arena.

Over the years, rodeo stock providers have developed sophisticated breeding programs to allow them to breed horses specifically to buck. Some of the finest bucking horses in the world of professional rodeo are products of these "Born to Buck" programs. Broncs are not mean aggressive horses, in fact they are nice natured when being handled on the ground.

They are just like any other horse, with one exception.
They really really don't like being sat on when a rider climbs on his back.
His one goal in life is to BUCK him off, as fast as possible.

Why ride for only 8 seconds?

The 8-second qualified ride was devised purely for the safety and well being of the animals involved. After 8 seconds the horses bucking ability decreases because of fatigue, adrenaline loss, etc.

The buzzer or horn will sound to signal the rider to end the ride and prepare to dismount.
This keeps the animal's spirit high The object is not to "break or tame" the bronc. For this same reason horses are not over used in a season. Its a pretty good life, their work day is only 8 seconds long.

What is wind-sucking and why is it a problem?

Wind sucking is classified as a stable vice

The horse will latch onto a fence post with his teeth (mouth open) and gulp large quantities of air. This habit becomes addictive.

Each time they suck and gulp the air, they receive a hit of endorphins which is similar to a drug, hence the addiction.

The wind sucker is often under weight and mal-nourished because of this incessant desire. They fill their stomachs with air so they look bloated but there is nothing to nourish their bodies.

The habit is generally caused by boredom or from copying other horses do it.

Do Horses cry?

Horses don't cry for emotional reasons. It is usually due to dust or some other irritant in the eye and the tear ducts are flushing it out.

Excessive tearing may be due to infection and needs medical attention.

Do horses get hiccups?

Horses can get huccups just like us, but it is very rare. Equine hiccups sound more like a cough. You will see the whole body twitch in spasm. The condition has been called the "Thumps" ever since 1831 when a British vet heard the characteristic thumping noise in the horses abdomen

What is equine "Self-mutilation" and why would a horse deliberately harm himself?

This behavior commonly known as flank biting, mostly afflicts stallions who are kept in isolation and away from estrous mares, usually housed in a dark corner of the barn with little or no turn out. A stallions natural function is to breed and protect his mares. When this natural function is denied a build up of testosterone causes frustration.

His frustrations can manifest in self-mutilation because there is no one else to take out his frustrations on, so his anger turns inward.

In addition to biting his flanks and chest, the horse will show seemingly uncontrollable violent behavior, which may include spinning in circles, bucking and kicking, causing injury to himself.

The cure is to rectify the cause and allow the stallion to live in a pasture with a few brood mares. Or as many horse owners resort to - have him gelded which always resolves the issue.

When does a colt become sexually aware?

The popular belief is that a colt starts to become sexually aware at around two years of age. He will be interested in mares and may become more aggressive when mares are around.

Younger colts have been known to breed with mares and produce foals, but these are usually u planned and considered accidents.

I was shocked when I observed and photographed this 3 month old colt exhibiting typical stallion behavior.

Colts are obviously born with a very strong sense of who they are and what they are here for.

This foal was living in a large domestic herd of mares and foals.

The foal watched a mare poop then promptly went over to sniff it.

He then stood over the pile and urinated on it to make his claim and mark his territory.

Then he walked off, curling his lip in the air (Fleming) as he went

There was no stallion running with the herd, so he had not observed this behavior.

38

Do Horses have a "personal space"?

Yes they do, but that space varies with each horse.

The horse's comfort zone will vary depending on the circumstances and the horses past experiences.

Horses form friendships and bonds with other horses that they will allow into their personal space, however that close familiarity is not necessarily afforded to every horse in their herd or others they come in contact with.

Some horses have extreme reactions when their space is rudely entered. They may kick or bite at whoever the offender is which can be equine or human.

Other horses will instantly know from their body language that they are pushing their personal space boundaries.(All horses speak the same language)

Sometimes humans are not as quick to pick up on the "back off" signals. Many horses have learned to tolerate ignorant space intrusion by people while others may become even more defensive.

It is believed that when a horse reaches out and gently touches a person with its muzzle that permission is being granted to touch him.

To understand why horses Kick or Bite let us try and **Think like a Horse.**

Imagine a 12 year old girl running up to you squealing "Oh you are so cute I could eat you up" and planting a big kiss on your nose, or reaching up to fondle your ears.

Unless you were related to this child you would find this kind of behavior very disturbing. You would feel yourself backing off from her.

Or imagine a mature man coming up quietly from behind you and slapping you on the rear to get your attention. It certainly would get your attention, but not in a positive way, because in both scenarios your personal space was violated without permission.

However if either one of them had tapped you gently on the arm or shoulder to get your attention, it is likely this action would not cause you any discomfort and your response would be more positive.

This kind of personal space invasion happens to horses all the time.

Some horses tolerate, it but others will lash out.

Why dont all horses behave the same?

To answer this question we need to consider that all horses have different per-sonalities and temperaments which means they don't all think and react the same way.,

Just like people, the horse's personality is made up of the characteristic patterns of thoughts, feelings, and behaviors It is considered "his personality " when these traits are fairly consistent throughout his life.

Most equine behavior is learned behavior so understanding the difference be-tween learned behaviors and temperament can be very useful.

Studying a horse's personality type can help you understand why a horse behaves and reacts to stimulus in a certain way.

Of course no one can talk to the horse to know what he is really thinking so these personality groupings are based on observation.

The social horse is quite interactive and interested in the world around him. Social horses are the official greeters of the horse world. Even as youngsters, this type usually likes being petted and made a fuss over. They often enjoy playing with other horses through-out their lives. Social horses are the most likely to welcome you into their personal space, and they may be quite happy to invade yours. They are a pleasure to own, and more forgiving of poor handling than the other types.

The Busy horse has to be doing some-thing all the time. They are curious and thrive on lots of interaction with other horses and people. Boredom will drive them to be creative and invent things to do like chew the stalls, slide their teeth up and down the bars, pawing and banging the doors to get atten-tion. they tend to get themselves into trouble.

The Boss horse has a strong sense of self is prideful and arrogant, especially when young or still entire. He values his personal space, and may defend it aggressively. This confident horse is opportunistic and will take advantage of timid or inexperienced handlers.

The fearful horse is much more guarded and cautious especially when young. He often needs more personal space and may become stressed and panicky when confined or tied up. New situations and environments cause him anxiety. He often has quick reflexive-type reactions He is more likely to "flee" than "fight". He draws most of his confidence from a person or another horse he has bonded with.

The aloof horse
is not particularly interactive. Content to be in his own little world, he often seems independent of both people and horses.

The Work horse - They love to "work". Without hard work, they become difficult, as they have lots of energy. They are quick to learn and happy when they know what is expected of them. They tend to be more people orientated and have little interest in other horses.

This is a fascinating study. One could spend a lifetime
Watching Horses
and trying to unravel the
secrets of what makes them tick.

Do horses have good memories?

Oh Yea!

They have excellent memories, which is the reason we can train them to perform all kinds of tasks.

If they "lived in the moment" like some people choose to believe and had no recollection of what happened yesterday - last week or even last year,
you would need to re-train your horse anew, each time you wanted to ride him.

Just like people - when you teach a horse something today he will remember it tomorrow - the more you reinforce it by repetition, the more it will stay in his memory.

Do horses remember people ?

Again Yes

They remember if someone was kind to them and gave them treats - When they

Likewise if someone was cruel to them, it may take a long time for the horse to forgive and forget.
That person will have to work hard to re-gain his trust and earn any forgiveness.

Horses recognize people By their voice.

You can test this theory:
By calling YOUR horse from the field gate, he will look up. If he likes you, he may come over to visit.
Yet go to another field full of horses and call out to them - they won't recognize your voice so will just continue to eat. It's not that they are rude - but you are a stranger and typically horses don't talk to strangers.

They also recognize the way you walk and carry yourself and your scent. To further test the theory, walk into the field but don't say a word.

You will get the same response from YOUR horse.

The other horses may come up to you if you walk into their field, because they are inquisitive and you might have food.

Do they remember things?

Well they seem to remember if they are afraid of plastic bags, tarps, umbrellas, and all kinds of other "spooky" things. It takes them quite a while to realize these everyday objects are not out to kill them.

How do horses learn - from Humans

Although this book is really about how horses naturally behave and think, not "how to train a horse".I felt is was important to understand how horses figure out what humans want them to do.

Horses are known to learn from:

Habituation. This is when, after repeated exposure to a stimulus, the horse becomes used to it. His reaction diminishes or disappears. This may involve human interaction, it applies in the case of grooming and handling a youngster, but it also applies to anything in his natural environment, such as wind, snow, or hail.

Desensitization. Some horse are extremely sensitive to new objects and situations. So a gradual process of desensitization is required. The horse is allowed to get used to new stimuli in increments. A trainer, for example, will introduce a saddle gradually to a horse, backing off if the horse shows an un-favorable response. Done properly, a horse will learn to willingly accept new objects and challenges.

Pavlovian conditioning. This is where a horse becomes conditioned to give a particular response. For example, if a trainer who pairs the word "trot" with the flick of a whip to get a horse to move to a trot. Done consistently, the horse will eventually respond to the verbal cue without the need for the whip. The use of food for reinforcement or even use of the word "good" can be part of this conditioning process.

Operant conditioning. Horses respond well to this form of learning; it is a standard part of most training practices. When a horse begins to learn the meaning of a new stimulus, its response is initially random. Through trial and error, it will offer the desired response.

Positive reinforcement used at the right moment will encourage the horse to repeat the behavior.

Its repetition will be a little hit and miss at first, but with continued use of positive reinforcement, the horse will learn the cues and offer the response the trainer wants.

Do mares have a favorite foal?

This might seem like a strange question. After all mothers are supposed to love ALL their offspring equally.

Let me tell you about this particular mare and foal
My field research took me to a farm in Winfield to observe and photograph a herd of Pintabians these horses are 99% Arabian and 1% pinto.
The goal of the breeder is to produce colored young stock either black and white or brown and white depending on which stallion they were sired by.
As we were walking to the main pasture, I spotted a solid chestnut mare and foal in a small paddock and enquired about her. The foal was only 3 weeks old.
The owner was dissapointed that the foal was not colored but he told me that the mare was more loving and more protective over this colt than any of her other babies (who had all been black and white).
He said,
"it was because this baby
looked like her."
Which begs the question
Do horses know what they look like?
Well they do have good
peripheral vision and when they
are young they are very flexible
so they can see themselves
But what really
rocked my World was the thought
Are Horses "Self Aware"?

Are Horses "Self Aware"?

This was something I had never even considered before.

So I did what every self respecting researcher does – I Goggled it
to see if any research had been done to test self awareness in horses.

But my search came up blank – so I decided to devise my own equine self
awareness test using a large Plexiglas mirror.

It was a very simple test. The purpose was to determine if the horses would
recognize themselves in the mirror.

In the interest of continuity,
all the test subjects were stallions, who were usually housed alone in their own
pens away from other horses. So the normal day to day life would be very
similar between all the test subjects.

The Self Awareness Test

The mirror was placed in the stallion pen
with the back showing

The horse was allowed some time to
check out the new object in his pen
(until he lost interest in it).

The mirror was then turned
around so he could see his reflection
This is when the fun started.

After a while the mirror was turned
around again so the horse couldn't see
his reflection.

The test lasted around half an hour
The test was carried out with 12 different stallions,
and although it really doesn't answer the question are horses "Self Aware".
The experiment did show that horses do not recognize themselves in a mirror
which must mean they don't know what they look like.
Each horse we tested reacted in exactly the same way.

Can horses see their reflection in water?

Although horses have amazing peripheral vision they have two blind spots
one directly in front of his nose and the other directly behind his tail.

A horses eyes do not work like ours, because they are positioned on the side of
the head - his right eye Sees what is on the right hand side of the horse and his
left eye Sees what is on the left. **They cant see their reflection in water.**

When the mirror was first placed in their pen (mirror side to the wall) the horse went over to investigate this new item in his pen.
He sniffed it for a few moments but soon walked away.

Once the mirror was turned around and the stallion caught sight of his reflection - he was fully engaged.
His first reaction was one of aggression to this new horse in his pen. He snorted and repeatedly struck out at the mirror with his front feet to send a message to this intruder (his reflection).

However, his aggression was mirrored exactly by the other horse, so neither one was more dominant.
So his next action was one of submission.
He lowered his head and neck and sniffed at the feet of his reflection - this brought about a truce between the horse and his reflection and he wandered away from the mirror.

He then returned to attack the intruder once again - this cycle of aggression and submission went on for about 20 minutes.

The mirror was then turned around to face the wall again
The horse's reaction was - "where has that horse gone"?
He ran up and down the fence line looking for the other horse.
He tried looking over and behind the mirror in search of him.
He even called (neighed) out to the imaginary horse.

It was evident that all of our test subjects did not recognize the horse in the mirror as himself.

It was a fun experiment
but I still had this nagging question in my mind about the Chestnut mare and foal – why did she care more for this foal that looked like her?

Then I had a **light bulb moment**
A foal's first love is her mother
This is true of all mammals including humans.
It is Mom who feeds and nurtures her baby, she keeps her baby close and protects it from danger - This is especially true in those first few days of life.

So if the foal's Mother is a Chestnut - will that detail make the foal pre-disposed to like and gravitate to other chestnut horses as she matures.

Will Bay become her favorite color?

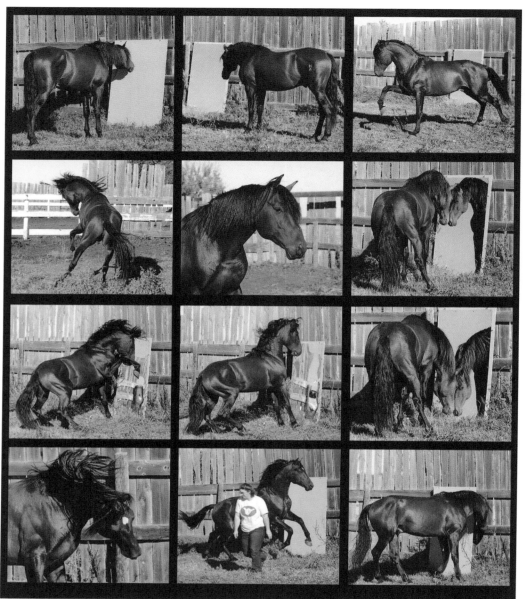

Horses have excellent memories,
Perhaps when a horse Sees a horse who resembled its own mother, in color and type, warm and fuzzy feelings are triggered.

Guess what, the Chestnut mares dam was also a Chestnut "Whoo Hoo"
Maybe we have discovered the missing piece of this puzzle.

After talking to other breeders to see if they had witnessed this phenomenon in their breeding stock, they confirmed there is definitely a pattern.
This is not an exact science, and there will be exceptions I am sure.
But we may have stumbled upon a key factor in understanding why horses form the friendships they do.

Do stallions follow a similar pattern?

Still thinking along the same line I started to wonder if the same was true for stallions.

The question I asked 50 stallion owners was:

Did their stallions have a color preference when it came to mares they liked to breed.

So the results would be unbiased I didn't tell them why I wanted to know.

Only after they described the likes and sometimes dislikes of their stud did I ask about the color of his Dam to see if there was any connection.

The results were very interesting:

Only 5 of the 50 studs showed a preference for mares that were the same color as their mother.
Which indicated there was no significant link.

However 85% of the stallions had a distinct preference for either Grey or palomino mares.

So maybe the rumor is true
Blondes do have more fun.

Point to ponder

Colts become sexually aware around 3 - 6 months of age, at which time he will cheekily try and breed with his mother.
She will most certainly chastise him for such rude and disrespectful behavior. In an attempt to teach him manners and how to behave around other females without getting seriously hurt.
Perhaps, as an adult stud, when presented with a mare the same color as his mother to breed with, he may remember his rejection and be a little wary.

A Healthy Horse is a Happy Horse

In this section we will look at some common, and some not so common questions regarding a horse's health and general well being.

Lets start with some of the basics

How many bones does a horse have?

The horse's skeleton not only provides a frame for the muscles and tendons to produce movement, but also protects the intenal organs. Bones are held together with ligaments, which allow movement but also prevent over-extension of the joints.

Most horses have 205

How many teeth does a horse have?

Foals get their first milk teeth shortly after birth; they keep these until the horse is about two years of age.

Then his permanemt teeth start to grow and push out the milk teeth.

Males have 40 teeth females 36

How big is a horses brain?

A horses brain weight about 23 ounces The human brain weights more than twice that.
However you cant measure equine intelligence by the size of his brain.

If you think your horse is stupid, he will outsmart you, and if you think he is smart - he will be as dumb as a sack of hammers.

What is the horses largest organ?

A horses skin is a huge and complex organ, which serves as a barometer for his inner health. Although we don't often think of the skin as an organ, it is in fact the largest organ in your horses body, and its importance to his overall health is staggering.
The skin is the first line of defence between the horse's delicate innards and the environment. It protects the rest of the body from physical injury and invasion from insects, micro-organisms and poisons.
It helps regulate the horse's body temperature through sweating.
The skin prevents the horse from dehydrating.
It excretes some unwanted toxins through sweat and also produces vitamin D from the sunlight.

Can horses see in the dark?

If you have ever called your horses in from the pasture after dark, you will no doubt have cringed as they came galloping towards you, but never stumble or bang into each other.

They may not see color as well as humans but their eyes are designed to pick up more light, so horses see pretty good in the dark.

If you have ever taken a picture of a horse using a flash, the horse will look like he has ghostly white eyes. This is caused by a membrane at the back of the eye that reflects light and helps his night vision.

Are Horses color blind?

A popular myth is that horses are color blind and only see in shades of Grey. This is not true they do see color.
However they only have 2 color receptors in their eye unlike humans who have 3. So they do see color, but not the whole color spectrum.

What is "Moon Blindness"

Moon blindness is the most common cause of blindness in horses.
It affects up to 12% of horses worldwide, however Appaloosas and quarter horses seem to be more vulnerable than other breeds.

The medical term is "Equine Recurrent Uveitis". It is thought that ERU develops in the wake of some other viral infection such as flu or equine herpes. But the exact cause of this disease is still under debate.
ERU attacks the eye causing blindness and ultimately dissolves the eye just leaving an empty eye socket.
This nasty disease also causes inflamation of the brain.

Why do some horses have blue eyes?

Blue eyes occur due to lack of pigment in the iris, most likely a result of **Double Dilute** coat color caused by the creme gene.
All double dilute horses have two light colored eyes.

Single dilute coat colors include palomino, buckskin, and smokey black when two horses carrying the creme gene are bred together. A double dilute foal is possible.

The first creme gene, works like the initial coat of whitewash over a dark wall, lightening the horse's red hairs from its original base color of chestnut, bay or black to palomino or buckskin.

The second creme gene acts as the second coat of whitewash making the horse's skin pigmentation and coat lighter in color.

The combination of two dilute genes affects the pigmentation of the horses eyes making both irises pale blue.

Are Blue eyes
More prone to disease?
No

Horses with blue eyes are no more at risk for general eye problems than their brown eyed relatives.

Blue eyes in horses are also commonly referred to as:

Wall eye - Glass eye or China eyes

Do carrots help improve a horses eyesight?

Carrots have long been reported for helping you see in the dark, so is this the reason horses have good vision? Carrots do provide Vitamin A, which is needed for healthy eyes. However horses get most of their vitamin A from grass.

How long do horses live?

The average life span of a well cared for horse is 25 - 33
Some live much longer
The oldest recorded horse lived to be 52

Donkeys enjoy a longer lifespan
          30 - 50 years
The oldest recorded donkey was called Flower. She lived to be 70 years of age.

It is unsure how long wild horses live.

50

What are a horse's "vital signs"

It is essential that every horse owner knows his horse's vital signs
Temperature - a horses normal body temperature is 99 - 101 f.

Pulse - the normal pulse rate is taken by listening to the heart on the left hand side of the chest just behind the elbow and is 36 - 42 beats per minute.

Respiration - the normal rate for horses is between 8 - 12 breaths per minute.

Do horses eat vegetables?

Although horses are herbivores (plant eaters) not all fruits and vegetables are good for horses in fact some are toxic.
These include:
Avocado - Onions - Garlic - Rhubarb Peppers - Broccoli - Cauliflower and Cabbage.
Also, feeding grass clippings to horses is extremely dangerous. The clippings ferment too quickly causing gas colic.

Do horses get toothache?

Yes, just like humans, horses need regular dental care and maintenance

How do you know he has toothache?

A sign that your horse has a toothache will appear initially as a training issue. He will toss his head in the air and avoid contact with the bit.

You may notice excessive drooling accompanied by bad breath, due to tooth decay.
Any infection around the tooth will cause painful swelling, causing the horse to become head shy and not let you touch his muzzle.

A normally good eater suddenly starts leaving his food and have trouble chewing. As a result he may lose weight.

What is Colic?

Colic is a general term for equine stomach ache.

The severity and symptoms will vary depending on the type of colic and what caused it.

Colic must be take seriously as certain types of colic can be fatal.

Can horses vomit?

Horses have a strong band of muscles around their esophagus.

This band is so strong that a horse's stomach would literally burst before it would allow any food to be regurgitated.

Its physically impossible for a horse to vomit.

Why do horses get "diarrhea"?

The equine digestive tract is complex and delicate system which is easily disrupted.

The most common cause of diarrhea is a change in diet, followed by stress. However more serious causes may be due to a bacterial infection or inflammation of the bowel.

Diarrhea affects both domestic and wild horses.

What different types of colic are there?

Impaction Colic

One cause of equine colic is an impaction. An accumulation of sand, dirt, feed, or other indigestible material obstructs the horse's colon, making it difficult or impossible for the horse to poop.

This form of colic, is a direct result of what the horse eats.

Gas Colic

Also referred to as spasmodic colic, it is exactly what it sounds like, It occurs when excess gases or fluids build up and create pressure within the horses stomach. It is extremely painful but the least serious type of colic and usually resolves itself with exercise - the horse can "walk it off".

Gastric Rupture

Gastric rupture, or a rupture of the stomach is relatively rare.

Enteritis

Enteritis is simply the inflammation of the intestine. The inflammation can be caused by many things, including infection, bacteria, and viruses.

Twisted Gut

The two most lethal types of colic are a twist in the gastrointestinal system of a horse and Intussusception (when the intestine slides back into itself, causing blockage). In both cases the blood supply may be cut off, resulting in dead tissue, that prevents food from passing through the gut and out the other end.

Enteroliths

This specific type of impaction colic is caused by naturally-occurring mineral deposits. They are stone-like formations. These stones can grow as large as 10-15 pounds. They typically form in the large colon but can migrate to smaller areas where they cause problems including colic. Enteroliths seldom completely block the passage of feed through the digestive tract.

Sand Colic

Sand colic is a type of impaction that occurs when a horse grazes on grass in dusty soil, often collecting upwards of 30-80 pounds of sand and dirt in its gut before colicking. Horses in sandy regions are more at risk from this type of colic.

What does a horse weigh?

The table below is an approximate guide to a horse's weight by height

Body Weight	Kilos
11hh	120-260
12hh	230-290
13hh	290-350
14hh	350-420
15hh	420-520
16hh	500-600
17hh	600-725

Which is why it really hurts when a horse stands on your foot!

How big is a horses heart?

It depends on the size of the horse of course, but on average a horses heart is the size of a basketball and weighs in at 8-9 pounds.

Did you know?

A thoroughbred's heart is proportionally larger usually weighing just over 1% of their body weight.

How fast do a horse's hooves grow?

The horse's hoof grows from the coronary band down towards the toe at an average rate of 1/4 to 3/8th of an inch per month.

The average hoof is 3 - 4 inches long.

This means the hoof is completely re-grown in a year.

The rate of growth is twice as fast in foals and horses under 1 year of age.

Just like most things in nature hooves grow faster in the pring and slow down over the winter.

Are black hooves stronger than white hooves?

There is a common myth that black hooves are stronger and less likely to split and crack than white hooves.

Science has proven there is no difference in the structural integrity of a white hoof compared to a dark hoof. The only difference is the lack of pigment. The texture and quality is the same.

What is Laminitis?

Laminitis is inflammation of the laminae of the foot, which is the soft tissue that attaches the coffin or pedle bone to the hoof wall. The inflammation causes extreme pain and leads to instability of the coffin bone in the hoof. In severe cases it can lead to complete separation and rotation of the bone within the hoof wall. Initially you will see rings forming on the outer hoof wall and as the disease progresses a complete sinking of the hoof.

Laminitis is a crippling condition. Once a horse has had an episode of laminitis he is particularly prone to future episodes.

Little fat ponies are more at risk especially in spring, when they tend to gorge on the sweet new grass.

Why do horses develop "Splints"?

The splint bones are small bones about the size of a pencil at the top and tapering down towards the bottom. They are found on each side of the cannon bone.

Sometimes a splint will "pop" causing a slight bulge at the side of the cannon bone. This happens when the splint becomes detached from the cannon bone. Initially the horse will feel pain, but once the splint bone has set or healed the horse will feel no discomfort.

Splints are caused by trauma or in balance.

Do Horses get the flu?

Yes - equine flu is caused by a virus which spreads in much the same way as human flu. It is transmitted through airborne particles,so allowing an infected horses to sniff another nose can spread the virus. The flu can also be passed from horse to horse by sharing buckets, troughs in fact anything that can carry the virus. It can quickly spread through an entire barn. The symptoms include runny nose, coughing, loss of appetite and fever.

Flu shots are now available for horses

Did you know?

Horses require around 1-2 ounces of salt per day.
In hot climates this requirement can increase to 4-6 ounces.

Salt licks and mineral blocks provide the perfect opportunity for domestic horses to consume what they need.

Wild horses rely on nature to provide them with the salt and minerals they need, by occasionally eating dirt or licking the ground and rocks.

What is Strangles?

Strangles is a highly contagious disease that attacks the glands in the horse's head and neck.
The strangles bacteria causes abscesses to form in the glands which become swollen and very painful. Sometimes the bacteria spreads to other organs causing abscesses. This is known as "Bastard strangles"
The infected horse will have a temperature, swollen glands and a nasal discharge. He will be very ill for up to 3 - 4 weeks.
Most horses make a full recovery but in severe cases it can be fatal.

There is no vaccine to prevent strangles.

Do Horses get warts?

Yes - but equine warts are fairly harmless. They are caused by papillomaviruses. The virus is transmitted by direct contact with infected items such as bedding/blankets etc.

Clusters of warts occur mostly on horses under two years of age. Older horses build up an immunity to the organisms that cause them.

Equine warts are small raised lumps which can appear anywhere on the body, although the muzzle is the most common location. They almost always just disappear on their own.

Don't worry you cant catch equine warts - they do not transfer to humans.

Do horses drool (like a dog)?

They shouldn't.

A drooling horse is cause for concern. He may have "Horse Saliva Syndrome" which is a fungal infection.

This particular fungus lives in the roots of red clover; the fungus releases an alkaloid called slaframine, which causes the salivary glands to work over-time, Symtoms include :

drooling, difficulty breathing, diarrhea and increased urination.

Once the cause is removed, the condition usually clears up.

What is Quidding?

If you find wet lumps of partially chewed hay or grass (that looks a bit like a birds nest) in your horse's stall or pasture. Thats quidding, it happens becauseIt is the horse is unable to fully chew his food, most common-ly caused will be dental problems. Sharp, overgrown, broken or missing teeth can impair the way a horse eats. Infected gums or abscesses may also be to blame .These lumps are called "Quids". Quidding may cause the horse to lose weight, because he is not getting the nutrition he needs.

What does it mean when a horses whistles and roars?

The terms whistling and roaring are used to describe horses that make abnormal respiratory noise during exercise.

The noise is heard when the horse breaths in and may sound like a soft whistle right up to a harsh roar.

The cause is anything that interferes with the passage of air. Which is most commonly damage or paralysis to the larynx.

This problem gets worse over time and the only solution is a surgical procedure called "Hobday" to open up the airway.

What does "Broken Winded" mean?

Horses can get COPD Chronic Obstructive Pulmonary Disease, which is also known as Equine Asthma- Heaves or Broken winded.

It can be caused by dusty or moldy hay, dust, or pollens in the bedding.

Symptoms are coughing, labored breathing and a yellow nasal discharge.

In severe cases, the horse appears listless, has difficulty breathing and develops a muscular "heave line" along the horse's barrel from taking double exhalations to push the air from his lungs.

What is a Rig?

A true rig is a male horse that is carrying either one or both testicles concealed in his abdomen.

Visually he appears to be a gelding, yet he behaves like a stallion.

These horses are medically described as a "cryptorchid" literally meaning hidden testicle.

What are the signs of a Healthy Horse?

A healthy horse is alert and inquisitive, happy to interact with other horses (sociable) he partakes in normal herd behavior such as mutual grooming sessions, snoozing throughout the day and running around with the herd.

A healthy horse will have a good appetite and roll occasionally.

A healthy horse will pass manure 8-12 times per day with the color and texture varying depending on his diet. His urine will be clear or slightly cloudy and is passed without any signs of discomfort or strain.
His coat will be smooth and shiny.

What signs let you know a horse is sick?

It is important that you recognise the tell tale signs that your horse may be sick or injured, so you can investigate further and take appropriate action. Watch for a change in his normal behavior:

* Standing around with his head hanging low
* Not joining in with the herd
* Laying down more than normal - or not at all
* He may look tucked up - the area behind the ribs appears to be sucked in
* Anxious behavior and sweating - a horse doesn't sweat unless he has good reason. Either it is very warm weather, he's just been worked or has been running around with the other horses.
* Looking at his flanks, and pawing the ground, repeatedly getting up and down / rolling (all signs of abdominal pain)
* Yellow or green sticky mucus in the nose or nostrils
* Unusual aggressive behavior
* His coat is standing up
* He may pass runny manure or may not pass any or strain to pass urine. The urine also may be a funny color

Learning to recognize these signs may be the most important job of the horse watcher.

What goes in must come out

I know the focus of this book is watching horses
But **did you know,** you can tell a lot about your horse's health by examining his poop. If you consider manure production to be one of a horse's vital signs along with normal temperature, respiration and heart-rate, then it is important to know what his "normal poop" looks like.
Any variation can be the first warning signs that something is going wrong.

Too Moist - Sometimes this may be due to stress or excitement but diarrhea can indicate the onset of a viral infection or inflammatory bowel disease.
But first rule out any obvious causes like a sudden change in diet.
Too Dry - Constipation does not typically happen to horses If it does it normally falls under the impaction type of colic category. Usually the cause of dry manure is lack of water. Horses need 5 - 10 gallons per day.
Color - also plays a role but greatly depends on what the horses has been eating. Alfalfa results in very green balls - beet pulp can leave the manure looking slightly reddish.
The two colors you really don't want to see are **red and black**. This could Indicate bleeding in the intestinal tract so it would be wise to call the vet.

Poop and Parasites

Any discussion on poop must include at least a token discussion of internal parasites. They can change the consistency of the manure. Parasites spend time in the manure as part of their life cycle.

They are very small and you may not be able to see them.
Roundworms, strongyles and tapeworms can cause a variety of health issues such as chronic diarrhea, weight loss, poor coat or even colic.

Managing internal parasites is an important part of horse management.

Internal parasites are also a problem for wild horses, who are not on a regular de-worming program. Wild horses graze over a large sometimes harsh terrain, which helps to control the parasite population.

Dental issues

If you notice large undigested food particles such as whole grains, this can be an indication that the horse is not chewing his food properly and may have problems with his teeth.

Ok no more potty talk I promise!

59

Horses have 5 primary senses
Sight -Sound -Touch -Taste and Smell

All these senses are far more acute and sensative than our own, but let us think about the horses sense of smell for a moment. if we can get a better understanding of how this works we will gain a whole better understanding of the horse in general.

There are dozens of ways horses use their sense of smell.

To identify friends, mares will deeply inhale the scent of a new foal so she will be able to identify him in the herd. A stallion will use his sense of smell to seek sexual relations, recognise territory, find appetising food or sense danger. It is also thought that they can smell death.

A Sharper Image - Photography

Nasal Anatomy

A horse has large nostrils which can flare to draw in more scents and chemical messages from the air. These pass over his olfactory receptors - millions of elongated nerve cells located in the upper portion of the nasal cavity, which are designed to analyze the smells.

Horses have a second pair of olfactory organs called the VNO's that have their own pathway to the brain. They function almost as a separate sensory organ. They come into play when a horse smells something, then curls up his lip in the air. This action is called Flehmen.

Stallions tend to do this the most, especially in the presence of a mare in season. They may flehmen several times an hour, checking for hormones in the air.

Mares will also Flehmen although not as frequently. Often the smell of birthing fluids will trigger the reaction.

While sex pheromones are definitely the most likely Flehmen trigger, they are not the only ones. Horses might react this way when confronted by unusual or pungent smells like smoke from a fire or fresh paint.

What smells attract horses and what smells repulse them?

Wouldn't it be great if we could identify which scents were attractive to horses, which fragrances put them as ease and helped them to relax?

And like wise what scents put them on full alert - induced fear and anticipation.

The only way to find out was to conduct an experiment:
So armed with a bag of essential oils I headed out to the stables
The experiment was quite simple
A few drop of each oil were sprinkled on a cloth and placed on a tub. The tubs were arranged in a large circle in the indoor arena.
The horse was led on a loose rein to each tub and allowed to sniff the cloth.

We were paying close attention to his body language, his ears, his eyes, his lips and nostrils - sometimes the reactions were subtle other times it was very obvious the horse disliked the smell

The oils used were:
Peppermint
Ylang Ylang
Jasmine
Green Apple
Anise
Lavender
Eucalyptus
Some fragrance we thought might have been familiar and others which might have be new to the horse.

The results
The experiment was carried out on 50 horses (various ages/ sex and breed)
The outright winner - the scent that every single horse loved was
Anise closely followed by peppermint.
The scents that were the least popular in fact some horses only took one sniff and turned their heads and bodies away from were the floral scents
Lavender and Jasmine.

This was a small test with only seven fragrances, but I know what perfume I WON'T be wearing next time I go out Horse watching - the florals will definitely be staying at home.

What is Ringworm?

The name sugests that this form of skin condition is caused by a worm.
But ringworm is caused by a fungus that lives on warm moist surfaces like the horse's skin. Ringworm is highly contagious and will happily live on horses, dogs and humans.
The fungus forms circular lesions that cause the hair to fall away, leaving an inflamed crusty patch. These patches spread quickly, are unsightly and cause the horse discomfort. An antifungal wash that kills the spors is the best treatment.

Do horses get sunburn?

It is very common for horses with white faces to get sun burned especially around the muzzle where there is less hair to protect the pale sensitive skin. Sunburn is just as painful for horses as it is for humans and shows up in much the same way.

Red, raw skin, hot to the touch which may blister if left untreated.

What causes a horses "Heel" to crack? *Wet conditions and mud*

Cracked heels, also known as mud fever are a result of wet conditions that cause the delicate skin on the backs of a horses pastern, just above the heel to crack and become infected. It happens because of, any number of fungus or bacteria living in the mud.
The cracking leads to bleeding, crusty scabs and scarring. They are very difficult to cure because of the constant movement of the pastern.
The treatment is to keep the lower legs dry and apply a zinc based cream designed for diaper rash to keep the skin pliable as it heals.

Can horses get Malaria from Mosquito's?

The simple answer is NO.
However mosquito's can transmit EEE "Eastern Equine Encephaltis"
It is a rare disease that is caused by a virus spread by infected mosquito's, that causes inflammation of the brain

West Nile Virus

This is a mosquito borne virus that also causes inflammation of the brain and spinal cord in horses.
There is no cure for west nile virus.
Over one third of horses who contract the disease die.
Horses that do recover may still exhibit permanent neurological symptoms.

Why do horses rub their tails?

A condition called sweetitch might be to blame.
It is caused by a biting insect that likes to live in the horses mane and tail.
Some horses have an allergic reaction to the bites, causing inflammation and intense itching.
Affected horses will rub their manes and tails till they are bare and sore. But they get no relief from the itch.
Treatment is difficult because it is unknown exactly what is causing the allergic reaction.

Why do Horses get worms?

This is a huge and complex topic, but the simple explanation is:

Most (but not all) internal parasites/ worms that affect horses are the result of grazing on contaminated grass.

The horse eats the grass containing eggs or larvae - these pass into the gut - or travel to other internal organs, where they stay and feed off the horse. They can stay in the horse for months, even years before erupting into full grown worms. At that time they will allow themselves to be swept along with all the other waste material and pooped out back into the pasture so the whole cycle can begin again.

There are many types of worms including:

Large red worms, Large round worms, Pin worms, Lung worms, Hair worms, Thread worms, Tape worms and Bots.

A heavy infestation can cause the horse to lose wight and condition.

Whats the big deal about Bot flies?

You may have seen large clusters of yellow eggs clinging to horses front legs during the summer months - these are Bot fly eggs.

They wait for the horse to rub or lick his legs, perhaps to relieve an itch.

Instantly the eggs, spurred by the moisture and warmth of the mouth, hatch into pinhead-sized larvae which sets about burrowing into the gums.

There they grow to about 5-6 mm After about 3 weeks they release their grip and travel down the horse's throat to the stomach and attach themselves to the gut wall - where they live for 10 months

Large infestations can cause damage to the stomach lining , ulcers and colic.

Eventually they release their grip and emerge in the dung where they hatch into fully grown Bot flies and the cycle starts again.

What about external (crawling, blood sucking) Parasites?

Mites, are harmless, right?

These tiny parasites use stealth to attack their prey.

Some mites lay their eggs on the ground - others on the horse. Their eggs stick to everything and once attached to a host they quickly hatch and begin feeding on the skin or in some cases burrowing under it causing "**Mange**".

Mites are highly contagious and can infect humans through contact with either an infected horse or his equipment. Mites lurke in blankets and tack just waiting for a warm body to come close.

What are Ticks?

Ticks are a blood-sucking (beetle-like) parasite that attacks horses, cattle, sheep in fact any animal it can attach to including humans.

They live in the long grass. When a possible host passes by they attach themselves by burrowing their heads into the victims skin. They suck blood until their body is full, then they drop off to develop into the next nymph stage. Ticks need blood to complete each stage in their development.

Ticks are not contagious, but they do spread a variety of diseases including Lyme disease.

Do horses get "Lice"?

Lice are small wingless, insects usually 3mm long. Their claws and legs are adapted to cling to long hairs. Thicker winter coats create an ideal living condition for them. Lice are the most common equine parasite. If a horses has lice, it's likely he will have what looks like heavy dandruff and greasy skin.

Blood-sucking lice like to live in the mane and tail, along the head and neck and also on the inner thighs. Once attached, they reproduce rapidly, laying eggs that quickly develop into full grown insects the whole generation cycle is completed in 4 - 6 weeks.

Severe lice infestation can cause anemia.

Wild Horses

The purpose of my study was to compare the behavior of domestic horses to that of "Wild Horses". To determine if man had changed horses natural way of being.

Alberta is home to two different breeds of wild horses.

A small herd of Przwalski's horses which are the last surviving sub species of wild horse are being bred in captivity at the Calgary zoo ranch. Plus there are a few hundred horses living wild in the foothills around Sundre, Alberta. Some folk believe these to be native wild horses that have been around long before European settlers came to the West. Others claim they are feral, once domestic horses used in the mines in the early 1900's. When the mines ceased operations, the horses were turned loose in the foot hills to fend for themselves.

The Przewalski's Horse

Where did they come from?

They were discovered in the late 19th century by a Russian explorer N.M. Przewalski, he found them living wild on the steppe along the Mongolia-China border.

Has 66 chromosomes
Domestic horses have 64

They are an endangered species with only 1,500 in existence. Most live in zoos but attempts are being made to re-introduce them to the wild.

Przewalskis are very herd orientated and do not mix well with domestic horses.
They are extremely aggressive. When they come into contact with domestic horses, they will kill the geldings and steal the mares to add to their herd. Despite the difference in their genes they will breed with the mares.
This not only diluted their gene pool but also made them very unpopular with the farmers who hunted them to near extinction.

These little horses have never been tamed. They are truly wild and cannot be handled, haltered, or mounted. Their enclosure is surrounded by an 8 foot steel mesh fence. If they can reach the top of the fence while standing on their hind legs, they will be able to get over it. This is quite impresive since they only measure between 12 - 14 hands high.

In the wild they live in family groups of a stallion and his harem. The young males will live with the family until they are around 5 years of age, at which time they will leave in search of their own mating partners.

They do not form bachelor groups.

The young stud will wander around existing harems until he feels ready to challenge the dominant stallion.
When he does, a long fierce battle take place which can last for days.
However once a harem stallion is beaten it will take a long time for the mares to comply with the authority of the conquerer.
It's not a done deal.
Some of the mares will leave with their young and join another group.

66

Canadian Wild Horses

There are four main herds of horses living wild in Canada today.

A protected colony of horses on Sable Island in Nova Scotia.

Two herds in British Columbia's "Brittany Triangle" (Chilcotin)

One in the Sundre, Alberta (Rocky Mountain foot hills).

There are groups of people fighting to save the wild horses in Alberta and their right to live wild and free. However, there are Government agencies who want to see them gone so they authorize culls and round ups.

What do Wild Horses eat?

Nature provides the horses with a varied diet of wild grasses, roots, shrubs and plants. They obtain salts and minerals from the soil and fresh water from mountain springs and streams.

Why "Wild Horses" never need to diet

In nature, it is more advantageous to carry a little extra fat, because this will see animals through times when food is scarce during the winter.

Carrying a little extra weight is also a sign of good health, making a horse more attractive to the opposite sex. Only humans think skinny and malnourished is sexy.

Wild horses live a nomadic life; they are continually on the move in search of food.

We can learn a lot from their lifestyle
Fresh Air + Exercise and a natural diet = no need to diet

Do Wild Horses self medicate?

Yes - they will lick the powder of the side of **White Poplar** trees - it is a natural pain killer.

The powder carries the main ingredient from which Aspirin is made. Somehow wild horses know that:

Dandelion leaves and roots are good for the liver, kidneys and digestion

Wild Garlic is extremely effective in cleansing cholesterol from the blood. It stimulates the digestive tract and kills worms and parasites.

Willow is a natural anti inflammatory and helps relieve arthritic pain.

Nettles are rich in iron and vitamin C and aide circulation, making them ideal for laminitis and arthritis.

Why do horses hang out in herds?

All horses both wild and domestic crave the company of other horses.

In the wild, there are two kinds of groups or "bands". They are referred to as family groups and bachelor groups.

A lot has already been said about the dynamics of a family group, so let's focus our attention on the bachelors.

What is a Bachelor group?

When the colts become sexually aware (usually around 2 years of age) and try to breed with mares within the family group - the dominant stallion will drive them out.

At that time they are known as bachelor stallions. They will join up with other bachelors for safety and companionship.

This "boys' club" is just what it sounds like, carefree young studs on the cusp of adulthood running around together rolling in the mud and having fun.

Occasionally they will engage in play fights to home their skills for the day they attempt to challenge the dominant stallion and claim his family group.

Life is pretty good; they have no responsibilities, no mares to protect or territories to guard. Just "eat sleep and be merry" as the saying goes.

I spent over 60 hours in the foot hills observing the behavior of the wild horses to learn more about these bachelors.

I had one burning question that no one could answer.

Not all the young studs will aspire to challenging the dominant stallion. Some will steal a mare and start their own family unit.

My burning question was

How do they do that?

After all, the stallion is
always watching.

Which mare do they go
after
an older one who may
not get much attention
from the stallion any
more,
or a young filly?

The Answer will knock
your socks off!

The bachelors work as a team

During the Spring and summer when the mares are in heat ALL the bachelors in the group will be feeling a rush of testosterone and have only one thing on their minds - that is, to find a mate and breed.

So they will follow the family group - stressing the stallion and generally being a nusiance. When the urge becomes too great, they decide to move in and steal a mare.

The stallion can only chase off one stud at a time - so when he is chasing one horse, the other bachelors are bullying a young filly from the herd. She will be scared and outnumberd, so in order to survive, she goes with them.

The boys will then fight it out between themselves to determine who has the right to breed with her.

The filly will stay with the bachelor group until one stud claimes her as his, at which time they leave together to start a family.

Team work

Requires communication, co-operation, and a game plan.

If wild horses can work as a team so can domestic horses, (an interesting thought)

after all

Horses all speak the same language.

Did you know

Bachelor groups create "stud piles", which is quite interesting as they don't have a territory to protect.

Also, all members of the group will add to the pile. Unlike a family group in which only the dominant stallion will add to the stud pile.

How do horses protect themselves?

The wild horse's first choice is to flee from danger. They would rather take flight than fight. However, when cornered a horse will lash out physically and can be dangerous from both ends. He will use everything in his arsenal - biting, rearing, kicking, and striking out to drive predators away.

Domestic horses are typically docile under human care, however their defense mechanisms can sometimes be directed towards humans as an act of rebellion or attempts to escape harsh handling.

Who does the horse flee from?

It greatly depends on the location and which animals are native to that region. Here in Canada, horses can fall prey to:

wolves, coyotes, cougars, bears, and of course man

How good is a horses hearing?

A species that survives by getting a head start on marauding predators need a pretty good sense of hearing.

Horses constantly monitor the world around them, their ears flick back and forth continually listening.

They can take in the sound of a car driving by, a bird chirping, and a human approaching all at once from different places in the environment. The horse processes all that information and in a split second decides whether to react - all the while picking out the best blade of grass.

The process really is mind blowing and a key factor in his survival.
All his preditors run faster than he does, over a short distance.

Cougar	top speed	35 - 45 mph
Bear	top speed	25 - 30 mph
Wolf	top speed	35 - 40 mph
Coyote	top speed	35 - 40 mph

Wild horse has a top speed of 18 - 20 mph

Can you tame a wild horse?
Yes - many wild horses have been captured and broken to ride.
Once you have gained their trust, they make excellent riding horses. Many things you need to teach a domestic horse the wild ones already know; such as how to navigate a stream, jump fallen logs, pick their feet up in difficult terrain, and behave respect-fully around other horses. Some owners say they are smarter than domestic bred horses and quickly learn new tasks.

What colors do they come in?
The wild horses of Alberta come in a variety of colors.
Mostly Bay, Black, Chestnut, Dun and Grey roan.

However, there are a few Paints but no spotted (appaloosa markings) amongst the bands.

Do wild horses breed with domestic mares?
Yes - given the opportunity.
It is often said that the wild horses are just a band of unwanted "feral" horses. However it is highly unlikely that a domestic bred horse would survive in the wild.
A gelding would never be allowed to join a band, he would be kicked and chased away. Alone, he would be easy prey for wolves, cougars and bears.
An abandoned mare may get scooped up by a bachelor group if she is in season and willing to breed.

How big are wild horses?
The horses that live in the foot hills around Sundre, Alberta range in size from 12:2 hh to 14:2 hh.

They are a stocky little horse of a very distinct "type", quite unlike any other horses found in Alberta.

Who trims their hooves?

The wild horses never see a farrier, so how come their feet don't get over grown and cause lameness? The wild horses' nomadic lifestyle means they are continually moving in search of food. Their travels take them over rocky terrain, and the gravel logging roads, which naturally wears their hooves down. All this exercise keeps the frog soft and healthy as it pumps blood through the foot.

Nature

Did you know

In the winter, the wild horses will lick the salt off the road left behind by snow graders.

Do wild horses suffer from worm infestation?

The wild horses are not on a regular de-worming program, so you would think worm infestation would be a problem.

Not so! Their lifestyle is the key to their success and good health.

Wild horses cover 5 - 10 miles per day as they forage for food, grazing the thousands of acres of Crown land in the Sundre foot hills.

They are not forced to graze near poop - which is where the worm larvae live, naturally avoiding contaminated grass.

Domestic horses will graze the same pasture year round and continually re-infest themselves, due to their confinement and constant proximity to poop.

(Research the life cycle of internal parasites to understand how this happens).

Do wild horses get rabies?

If a horse is bitten by an infected animal they will contract rabies.

The virus replicates locally in muscle tissue, then travels up the nerves into the spinal cord and brain

The time between a horse being bitten and showing clinical signs can be 2 - 8 weeks. The horse will exhibit behavioral changes, fever, paralysis, and colic. He may have difficulty swallowing and eating.

Rabies is fatal.

There is a vaccine available for domestic horses.

How do horses stay warm in winter?

The horses grow long thick winter coats, which they can fluff up to trap warm air and retain body heat.

In the photograph below you will see a layer of snow on the horses back, an indication that no heat is escaping through his coat.

The mountain forest provides shelter and protection from sleet and heavy snow falls.

Do horses get frostbite?

It is very rare in horses but when it does occur, its likely to strike the ear tips. Frostbite strikes when tissue becomes frozen and ice crystals form inside cell membranes. Frost bitten tissues don't recover with thawing. Once they are dead they are dead.

Horses that can stay dry and find shelter from the wind and are allowed to acclimate to the cold gradually (as would normally happen with the change of seasons) can survive bitter cold temperatures of -20 - -40F quite nicely even for extended periods of time, as long as they have adequate food.

Do Horses eat snow?

Yes to get moisture when streams are frozen - however it is difficult for the horses to get enough moisture from snow, so dehydration can be a problem in the winter as moisture is lost through urine/ feces and breath exhaled from the lungs.

Answers to Questions you never knew you had

Have you ever wondered why horses do the things they do.
If only you could "Think like a horse", some of those things would make more sense.

What motivates a horse?

Horses really don't care about the "things" people care about. They see no value in ribbons and trophies. Motivation is described as the "desire or inner drive that causes an animal to do something"

Horses only have two goals:
One is to survive, the other
is to reproduce.
To go forth and multiply.

What causes horses to literally go crazy?

The Loco weed, also known as the crazy weed grows in the United States and is extremely toxic to horses. But unfortunatly very tasty - in fact horses can become addicted to it after only tasting it a couple of times.

The toxin in the plant causes problems with the nervous system resulting in: excessive salivation, aimless wandering, un-coordinated gaits, chronic weight loss, vision problems, infertility, and lethargy followed by extreme outbursts of energy.
The cure involves administering sedatives and laxatives while keeping the horse as calm as possible. The earlier the horse is denied access to the weed the better.

Can horses count?

Researchers have shown horses can count. By dropping apples one by one into two buckets, then allowing the horse to choose which bucket to eat from, researchers concluded that "Horses are Smart".
Not only do they have special social skills and an excellent memory, they can also count.

Most horses repeatedly chose the bucket containing more apples.

Can horses tell time?

There is no research to support it,
but horses certainly know when it's dinner time, and will let you know if you are late bringing their food to them.

Ask any instructor at a riding school if her lesson horses know when an hour has passed. I am certain they will all say the same thing.

The ponies know when they have done their time in the lesson.

Its like they are in some sort of workers union - quiting time is quiting time.

Do horses "fake" lameness?

Horses simply don't have the cognitive capability to plot and scheme in this manner. They just don't.

If your horse act lame, its because he is lame - call the vet.

In a similar vein, horses don't "spook" to annoy you or get the better of you or get out of work. Horses spook because something they see, hear, smell or touch has startled them and triggered a flight response.

Can all horses swim?

All horses are physically able to, but just like humans, some love it and others will avoid it at all costs.

When horses swim, they use their legs in a diagonal pattern much like when trotting but under water.

Swimming is a very strenuous activity for horses a 10 - minute swim is the equivalent of a several mile canter.

Can all horses jump?

All horses have the ability to jump to some degree. In the wild being able to jump a fallen log to escape a predator could be a life or death decision, so the ability to jump is a survival tool.

Some horses just do not enjoy the experience and would prefer to go around an object in their path rather than jump over it.

Also some breeds are more athletic and suited to jumping.

Horses are "Ungulates"

A horse is an ungulate,
which simply means it is a mammal
with hooves.
Horses have one hoof at the end of
each leg which makes them
odd-toed ungulates.
Cattle have two hooves at the end of
each leg making them even-toed
ungulates.

What is the difference Between a horse and a pony?

Size

horses and ponies are all equines
A horse is an equine that measures
14:2hh or greater.
A pony is an equine that measures less
than 14:2hh.

Why are horses measured in Hands Not feet?

Ancient horse traders needed a method
of measuring horses for sale.
Stacking one man's fist on top of
another was the simplest system.

Throughout history, human body parts
have been used as a means of
measurement

Over time, a foot became 12 inches
and a hand 4 inches.

Where do ponies come from?

Most ponies found in
North America are descendants of
British native ponies. These breeds
include:
Welsh - Cob, Section A and B
Dartmoor and Exmoor ponies
Fell and Dales
Shetland and Highland
Newforest
Connemara
Some were brought over by early
settlers. Others have been imported as
children's riding ponies in more recent
years.

What are Ergots and Chestnuts?

Chestnuts are hard callouses found on the inner side of a horses leg, above the knee on the foreleg and if present below the hock, on the hind leg.

Ergots are a similar callus but found on the underside of the fetlock. Some equines have them on all four legs; others have fewer or no detectable ergots.

In the scientific community chestnuts and ergots are generally accepted as the vestigial toes of Eohippus, an early ancestor of the modern horse that lived 50 million years ago.

Why do "Heavy Horses" have docked tails?

Draft and other breeds that are considered "harness horses" commonly had their tails docked (or amputated, both terms are correct) for two main reasons.

First, so the long hair would not get tangled in the harness and
Second, so the horse couldn't get his tail bone over the reins.
The underside of a horses tail is very sensitive. Reins or harness touching it may cause the horse to panic and bolt.

The practice has been banned in the British isles, Norway, parts of Australia and in eleven states in the USA.
However it is still seen on show and working draft horses in some places.

Objections to docking include concerns that the horse can no longer use its tail to swat flies, plus the pain and discomfort of the docking process.

Why do horses wear shoes?

Horseshoes were invented and applied more than 2,000 years ago.
Horse owners and cavalrymen began to realize that the work requirements of their horses were wearing their hooves faster than they could grow.
Horse shoes provide protection and traction to the horses' feet. They can be used to improve gait and aide soundness.

Can horses be cloned?

In general terms, a clone is an exact genetic copy of another individual.
In 2003, Italy's laboratory of reproductive technology created the first clone, a Hafflinger filly named Prometea. While the foal was born healthy, she was the culmination of 328 attempts.

Do horses
Get struck by lightening?

Horses that live outside all the time pay little attention to thunder storms. Amidst the crashing and banging, they just continue grazing.
But if the thunder is accompanied by driving rain, they will head towards trees to shelter from the rain.
This is probably the worst place possible: lightning can strike tall trees causing the electrical current spread to the animals sheltering underneath.

99% of the time lightening strikes to horses are fatal.
Cattle also share the same risk.

Do horses
suffer from allergies?

Just like humans, horses can and do develop allergies.
An allergy is an imbalance of the immune system resulting from reactions to grasses, tree pollens, food, or molds.

Equine allergies manifest either through the skin in the form of hives or sores, or in the respiratory system in the form of coughing and nasal discharge.
The best cure is to try to remove the cause.

Why do horses grow whiskers?

Whiskers play a very important role in a horse's life; these hairs are called vibrissae. They provide "feeling" for the horse around his muzzle.
He is able to sense whether something is hard, smooth, soft, sharp, hot or cold.
A horse's whiskers help him gauge the distance of objects to his face and muzzle. They help the horse avoid things that could possible injure him.
Whiskers are an extremely important sensory tool.

Why do some horses grow an abnormally thick coat?

Horses are expected to grow thick coats in the winter, but when they fail to shed their coats in the spring or grow a winter coat at an inappropriate time of year, it may be a symptom of cushings disease.
Common in older horses, Cushings disease is the result of a hormonal imbalance caused by a tumor found in the pituitary gland.
The coat of a horse with cushings may also be unusually curly.
There is no cure for equine cushings disease. Horses with cushings are also extremely prone to laminitis.

What is a "Grade" horse?

The term "grade horse" means a horse whose blood lines are unknown, unidentifiable, or of significantly mixed breeding. He is the "Mutt" of the horse world.
Not to be confussed with a cross bred. Crossbred horses are usually carefully planned to mix the desired attributes of two separate breeds.

Popular crossbreds that in time obtained their own breed registry are:
Irish spot horse
(Irish draft and Thoroughbred)
Anglo Arab
(Thoroughbred and Arabian)
Morab
(Morgan and Arabian)

What are geldings?

90% of male horses are not of breeding stallion potential, which makes the practice of "castrating" or gelding horses a popular solution.

Once the horses have been castrated, they produce less male hormones and become un-interested in mares.
this makes the horse suitable for a greater number of uses, plus he happily shares living areas and pasture with mares.

How many breeds of horses are there?
There are over 350 different breeds of horses in the world, but they all fall into Four main groups

Light horses - Horses with small bones and thin legs; some examples of light horses are Thoroughbreds, Morgans, Arabians, Warmbloods and Quarter horses
Heavy Horses - Draft breeds, heavier bodied with strong sturdy legs, some examples are Shire, Percheron, Clydesdale, Belgian, and Suffolk punch.
Ponies - Are no larger than 14:2 hands high; some examples are Welsh ponies, Shetland, Conemara, Fell, and Dartmoor.
Feral Horses - Horses which are wild or semi wild living free in herds. The Mustang, and horses on Baffin island would be examples of feral horses.

Do "Horse Flies" prefer white or dark colored horses?
Researchers have found that white horses were less attractive to blood sucking flies partly due to the polarization of light (white horses don't shine)

Dark horses are more attractive to horse flies, as their coats reflect more polarized light.

This is good news if you are a white horse.

Do Horses care what you wear?
With the vast array of specialty breeches, boots and jackets saddlery stores would like us to think so. But in reality horses really don't care if you are wearing a formal evening gown or jeans and a T shirt.

However, the most essential item of clothing when "Horse Watching" is a sturdy pair of boots.

How many colors do horses come in ?

There are 39, but more colors are added to the list all the time
The most popular colors are :

Bay, Black, White, Grey, Dun, Sorrel, Chestnut, Palamino, Champagne, Cremello, Perlino, Grulla, Buckskin, Strawberry roan, Blue roan, Brown, Pinto, Pearl.

Liver chestnut, Smokey grey, dapple grey, fleabitten grey, Skewbald, Piebald, Spotted, Tobiano, Blonde, Silver dapple, Brindle, Steel grey, Red dun, Leopard to name just a few.

What are Mules and Hinnies?

A Mule is a cross between a male donkey (called a Jack) and a female horse (mare)

Male mules are called Johns and females are called Mollies

A Hinny is a cros between a male horse (stallion) and a female donkey (Jenny) Mules and Hinneys are almost always infertile.

There is another cross that is becoming popular betweeen a Zebra and a Donkey called a ZeDonk or Zonkey and between a zebra and a horse which is called a Zorse.

What is the largest Breed of Horse?

The largest horses are the draft breeds. These horses were bred to pull or carry heavy loads Breeds include: Percheron, Clydesdale, Belgium, Suffolk punch,Bashkir, Italian heavy draft, Jutland, Noriker, Norman cob, Schleswig draft, Irish draft, Breton, Ardennais, Fjord, Haflinger The largest of them all is the Shire.

What is the smallest Breed of Horse?

The tiniest breed of horses is the Felabella, averaging only 25 - 34 inches measured at the wither.

Why do people tie ribbons on horses tails?

There are four different colors horse owners use to communicate different messages about their horse:

Red Ribbon - is a warning that the horse kicks, so give him plenty of room
Green Ribbon - Means the horse is young or inexperienced and likely to misbehave, again give him lots of room.
Blue Ribbon - Signifies that this horse is a stallion
White Ribbon - Means this horse is for sale

Why do Mules and Donkeys Hate dogs?

Donkeys and mules have deep rooted preservation skills. Coyotes, Wolves, cougars even our precious pet dog are all seen as predators to the donkey.

In his mind, pet dogs and wolves are both part of the same family so he takes a pro-active approach by attacking first and asking questions later.

Did you know

Donkeys originate from the desert areas of the world (Africa and the middle east). Because food is scarce in the desert their digestive system has adapted to break down rough grasses and shrubs that would be inedible to horses. Donkeys utilize 95% of what they eat with very little wasted.

Donkeys do not like to be out in the rain as their fur is not waterproof.

There are a variety of different breeds of donkeys (just like horse breeds).

Ethiopian Donkey - as the name suggests from Ethiopia, still commonly used as work animals, usually slate grey color.

Andaluz Donkey - Used by the Spanish military, a large donkey with excellent blood lines.

Catalan Donkey - their numbers were critically low in the late 20th century, but a breeding program has saved them from extinction.

Cotenin Donkey - found in Lower Normandie - once used to transport cow's milk. A breed registry was established for these donkeys in 1997.

Mammoth Donkey - is the worlds largest breed of donkey created by mixing blood lines. A strong animal capable of heavy workloads.

Miniature Mediterranean Donkey - found on the islands of Sardinia and Sicily, they are almost extinct in their homeland, but the Americans have taken a liking to them and saved the breed.

Parlag Donkey - From Hungary, he came there via the Celts and Romans.

Poitou Donkey - Thought to have been introduced to the Poitou region of France by the Romans - a large robust donkey with a very distinct thick woolly coat.

Zamorano -Leones Donkey - A Spanish donkey that was bred for transport and trade; later they were used to create large working mules.

Did you know

Donkeys hold the distinction in the Bible of being one of the earliest and most frequently mentiond animal in the text.

Jesus chose to ride a donkey rather than a horse when he entered Jerusalem as King of Kings.

Why do we lead and mount horses from the left?
Is it just tradition?
No - there is a science behind the practice. Recent research has shown that a horses left eye is the "rapid reaction eye" which simply means if a horses sees something he is unsure about - out of his left eye, his reaction to that stimulus will be stronger and a faster flight reaction than if the same stimulus was presented to his right eye.

Researchers found that most horses favored their left eyes and wanted to keep people in their left line of vision.

Early horse trainers probably noticed this and incorporated leading and mounting horses from the left as part of good horse training practices.

What is the difference between a Blacksmith and a Farrier?

A blacksmith is one who makes and repairs things made of iron or steel. It was the blacksmith who made and repaired items necessary for farming and daily living such as plows, axes, door hinges, logging chains, harness hardware etc.

A farrier is one who shoes horses, mules, and donkeys. He is an expert in equine hoof care and specializes in this area.
To further complicate things, in some parts of the world the farrier is also referred to as the blacksmith.

What is the purpose of "Hot Walking" a horse?
This is a term that refers to a person who is employed to walk a hot sweaty horse until he cools down naturally and his coat has dried. Usually a groom at a racing barn would have this task after a race or gallops on the track.

Why do we say Giddy up to encourage a horse to go faster but not Giddy down to make him go slower?
(I have no idea)

Why should one never look a gift horse in the mouth?
you can tell the age of a horse by looking at his teeth, but if he is a gift, it would seem rude to check if you have been given a youngster or an old nag.

Why do some horses have more than 4 gaits?

For simplicity's sake, the gaits recorded for horses are divided into two categories, natural and artificial.

Walk, trot, canter and gallop are the horse's natural gaits
Gaits such as the running walk, slow gait, pace, tolt and rack are considered artificial gaits.
However, these artificial gaits are very natural to specific breeds of horses. There are several breeds of gaited horses, with each breed possessing distinct gaits unique to that particular kind of horse. These horse have been selectively bred for movement, and over the generations of breeding these extra gaits have become natural to them.
Such breeds include the following:

American Saddlebred   Icelandic horse   Paso Fino   Peruvian Paso
Rocky Mountain Horse Standardbred   Tennessee Walker

The five-gaited American Saddlebred is shown at the animated walk, trot, slow gait, rack and canter. The slow gait and rack evolved from the breed's easy riding gait traits and showcase their brilliance and elegance.

Slow Gait - The slow gait is performed by the five-gaited Saddlebred; a four beat lateral gait is also known as the stepping pace. In this gait, the horse performs a broken pace, with the hind and front leg on the same side leaving the ground and landing at slightly different times.

Rack - The rack is a flashy, faster, more exaggerated four beat walk performed by the American Saddlebred and the Tennessee Walking Horse. Each foot meets the ground independently of each other.

Running Walk - is the gait characteristic of the Tennessee Walking Horse. This four beat gait is similar to that of the regular walk, yet faster. In the running walk the hind feet overstep the front foot print by as much as 18 inches. This travel gives the gait a gliding motion. The horse will bob and nod his head in rhythm with the his legs.

Pace - Standardbred Horses are driven in harness racing and can compete as trotters or pacers). Eighty percent of harness racing is performed at the pace gait, which is faster than the trot. The footfall pattern of the pace is the right hind and right front together, then left hind and left front together. As the horse rocks from side to side, there is a brief moment of suspension where all four feet are off the ground prior to the next lateral pair touching the ground.

Tolt and Flying pace - Tolt is performed by Icelandic horses and is similar to the running walk or rack of a Tennessee Walking Horse or Paso Fino.
The Tölt is a very smooth four-beat fast gait.

The Flying Pace - The hooves on the same side touch the ground together. the flying pace can equal the speed of a full gallop and is used in Iceland for racing. To Icelanders, riding at the Flying Pace is considered the ultimate in horsemanship.

Why do some horses get herd bound?

The number one cause for a horse to become herd bound is insecurity. If a horse does not feel safe or content within himself or in the world, of humans he will crave the security of other horses. His behavior will depend on his level of insecurity his behavior and his desperate urge to stay with his buddies.

Indications that he is herd bound are: Refusing to leave home, running towards home, rearing, spooking, all in an attempt to go back to his buddies. He may also repeatedly neigh and cry out to them.

What causes a horse to be insecure?

The causes of insecurity can vary. Foals are greatly influenced by their Dam's personality. A foal with a timid Dam may inherit (learn from her behavior and reactions) her timid nature. She keeps close to her side, becoming more and more dependent on her.

Foals with self-confident Dams on the other hand are often bolder and more curious, developing a strong independent attitude early in life. Horses learn from each other by example.

Perhaps a question to ask yourself is - Are you herd bound?

Some people are: if you always ride with someone else and go where they want to go. If you meet with friends on a regular basis and hate to be alone, if you need someone to always go with you to do something, like shopping or visiting new places. Even though you can rationalize why you shouldn't be, it is in your nature to want to hang out with your buddies and do things with a friend.

Maybe you are a little herd bound too. Which means, you can have a little more empathy with your horse.

So how much harder is it for a horse who is by nature part of a Herd ,to get over this insecurity and attachment?

What are some horse superstitions and old wives tales?

Some are funny some are ridiculous and some may hold a grain of truth
You can be the judge.

Horse brasses were supposed to protect horses from witches

Changing a horse's name is bad luck.

Eating hair from a horse's forelock is a cure for worms.

Horses standing with their backs to a hedge means its going to rain.

In England and Germany, dreaming about a white horse is an omen of death.

A horseshoe hung above the doorway will bring good luck to the home. In most of Europe, protective horseshoes are placed in a downward position - but in Ireland and Britain, people believe the horseshoe must be turned upwards or the luck will run out.

The "nail test" is thought to predict the sex of a mares foal. You must take a hair from the mares tail and tie a nail onto it. Then hold it above the mares hips ...if it doesn't swing she is not pregnant, if it swings in a circle its a filly if it swings back and forth its a colt.

Inhaling horses breath is a cure for whooping cough.

A horse who steps in a wolf print will be crippled.

If you put a piece of hoof trim in the microwave, it will turn into bubblegum

When a master dies, the horse will shed tears.

Grey horses and horses with four white feet are considered unlucky in racing.

Copper pennies placed in a mares drinking water will improve moody behavior.

What is Fact and what is Fiction?

The horse community is abound with tales, myths and country wisdom from folk lore to gypsy healing potions. In this section we will try and unravel the fact from the fiction.

Is Palomino a color or a breed?

The true meaning of "palomino" refers to the specific genetics and color of a horse. Genetically, a palomino is a horse that carries two red genes and one creme gene.

The creme gene lightens the red color into a golden yellow color with a lighter mane and tail. Palomino come in a variety of shades.

The reason it has been confused as a breed is because there are registries for palomino horses. However, these registries have restrictions on eligible colors and breeds.

Are there Albino horses?

The fact is, Albinism has never been documented in horses, however there is a condition known as the Lethal white syndrome that is often confused with albinism.

Lethal white syndrome is an autosomal genetic disorder that occurs most frequently with the American Paint horse breed.

Foals affected with this syndrome will be born with completely white coats and blue eyes. Although they look healthy and perfectly formed, very few of the foals survive. Death is caused by an underdeveloped part of the digestive system

Do horses sit (like a dog)?

Yes all horses adopt a sitting position; They just don't hold it for very long, because they go from lying down (when either sleeping of rolling) to standing up.

The horse will lift his front end up first, straighten out and lock his fore legs into a sitting position - then in a continuous movement haul his rear end up (it is not a pretty movement). Very often some grunting will be involved.

Sitting is uncomfortable for horses, plus difficult for them to muster the impulsion needed to raise their hind end. Some owners train their horses to do tricks, like bowing, rearing, lying down even sitting like a dog.

Is everyone who rides a race horse a jockey?

No - it is physically impossible for some people to ever become a jockey because size matters - jockeys must weigh no more than 126 lbs including all their equipment and tack.

Can jockeys race their own horses?

No - they are not allowed to own a horse that is being raced, but they do provide their own saddles/bridles/crops and other equipment.

Do jockeys just race one horse?

No - a jockey must be adept at managing and riding horses of different temperaments as he might ride up to 12 horses a day.

Do jockeys make lots of money

Most jockeys share a small percentage of the prize money if their horses win is usually around 5% but if it doesn't win, his fee is around $100

What is "The Jockey Club"

The jockey club is an organization dedicated to the improvement of Thoroughbred breeding and racing. Incorporated Feb 10 1894 in New York City, the Jockey club serves as North America's Thoroughbred registry, responsible for the maintenance of "The American Stud book" which is a register of all Thoroughbreds foaled in the USA, Canada, and Puerto Rico. And of all Thoroughbreds imported into those countries from jurisdictions that have a registry recognized by The Jockey Club.

What happens to a race horse when he retires from the track?

Most thoroughbreds are sold to private owners and are trained in new disciplines. Many go on to compete in dressage, show jumping and eventing.

A mare who has done well at the track may be used for breeding the next generation of race horses.

Why do all racehorses have the same Birthday - January 1st?

Because thoroughbreds all race according to age, giving them the same birthday eliminates confusion when entering races.

Foe example all horses born in 2010 will race as two year olds in 2012, regardless of when they were born in 2010.

Most Thoroughbred breeders try to breed so their foals are born as close to Jan 1st as possible (but not before) If a TB is born on Dec 31st, he is automatically one year old the next day.

Do Hot Blood and Cold Blood breeds have blood temperature differences?

No - the term hot blood or cold blood refers to the temperament as well as the breed of horse.

Hot bloods - are generally lean swift and excitable. These breeds include the Thoroughbred and Arabian.

Cold Bloods - This term is used exclusively for draft horses; they are known to have a calm, gentle, docile temperament.

Warm Bloods - Came into being by crossing cold blood and hot blood breeds to create a large sport horse. Breeds include the Hanavarian, Trakehner and Westphalian

Why is a Purebred not necessarily a Thoroughbred?

A Thoroughbred is a registered breed of horse whose origin may be traced back to records as early as the third century. These horses were selectively bred for speed and stamina.

A Purebred horse, is a horse that has two parents of the same breed and is registered with the appropriate breed registry.

What is a "Horse Culture"

A horse culture is a tribal group or community whose day to day life revolves around the herding and breeding of horses.

History offers many examples of horse cultures such as the Huns and other peoples in Europe and Asia. Our modern day equivalent would be the horse ranchers and breeders.

Horse cultures tend to place a great deal of importance on horses. By their very nature, they are nomadic and usually hunter gatherer societies.

For example the arrival of the horse in America revolutionized the culture of the Plains Indians, allowing native people greater mobility. Horses impacted every aspect of life including trade, hunting and warfare.

How many horses are there worldwide?

According to "Google" there are about 75 million horses in the world and 7 billion people.

I'm not sure how you could possibly count them all, but its a fun fact to share at parties.

Why are bad dreams called night mares?

The term nightmare has only been around since the mid 19th century. Before then the cause of a bad dream was blamed on a "Mera" an name used for Goblin.

What is a Charley horse?

It has nothing to do with horses. A Charley horse is a term used to describe a painful muscle cramp in the arm or leg, usually caused by strain.

Do horses like music?

Is music played in your barn? Ever wonder if the horses like it? In a recent study, researchers at Hartpury College in England found that horses liked classical and country sounds better than Jazz or Rock - they didn't say how they came to this conclusion.

91

How high can horses jump?

The official
Federation Equestre Internationale
record for high jump is:
2.27 meters (8ft 1.2 inches)
By Huaso Ex-Faithful, ridden by,
Capt. Alberto Larraguibel Morales.
This amazing feat took place in
Chile on Feb 5th 1949.

This is the exception not the norm.

What is a Schoolmaster?

This is a term used to describe a well
behaved and experienced horse. One
that has seen it, done it and got the
T shirt. "The perfect pony"

How fast do horses go?

The walk averages 4 mph.
The trot averages 8-12 mph.
The canter averages 12 - 15 mph.
The gallop averages 25-30 mph.

The World record for a horse
galloping over a short distance is
55 mph.

Linda Finstad
Fine Art Photography

What is Dressage?

Dressage dates back to the classical Greek horsemanship and the Military who
trained their horses to perform movement intended to evade or attack the enemy
whilst in battle.
The earliest dressage manual was written by Xenophon, a Greek military
commander around 430 BC.
During the Renaissance, European aristocrats displayed highly trained horses in
equestrian pageants.
The great horsemen of the time developed a training system, and the Imperial
Spanish Riding School of Vienna was established in 1572.

All dressage training today is based around their principles.
Dressage became an Olympic sport in 1912, however, only commissioned
Military officers were eligible to compete. It was only in 1952 that the rules
were changed to allow both civilian men and women to compete in the games.

Is Cat nip just for cats?

Did you know, Catnip is 10 times more effective to repel mosquitoes than Deet?
Catnip is an-easy-to grow perennial herb that thrives just about anywhere.

Use some of the leaves to make a low cost, all natural fly repellent.
Mix some of the crushed dried leaves with some water in a saucepan and
simmer for 15 minutes. Allow the liquid to cool and strain into a spray bottle
It is safe to use on yourself and your horse.
The best time to gather the leaves is just after they bloom usually between June
and September.

Do horses have a sense of humor?

Fun is one thing, though
"Funny" is another.
We all know horses (especially young-sters) love to play with each other and
with toys.

Horses will steal things - like your hat
and run off with it just for fun.
but do horses display humor or
behave in a way designed to get
reactions out of other horses just for
laughs?

There has been no scientific research to
prove they do.
So maybe this is a task for the "Horse
Watcher"; to uncover the truth.

The Jury is still out

Do horses have "Wisdom teeth"?

Some horses (not all) grow wolf teeth,
they are vestigial teeth, which means
they are no longer necessary. They
are often thought of a bit like wisdom
teeth in people.

Wolf teeth are positioned just in front
of the cheek teeth (back grinders)
usually on the upper jaw.

Wolf teeth can be problematic if they
interfere with the bit. The common
practice is to remove them.
But if they cause no discomfort to the
horse when he is being ridden (owners
are very often unaware their horses
have them) they are best left alone.

No one really knows why they are
called wolf teeth.

Do horses Mourn?

Death is obviously a part of life. Since horses are very relationship orientated and social, they crave and require companions of their own kind.

Some horses form extremly strong friendships with other horses. A horse without the company of other horses is a very sorry creature indeed.

They may not mourn in the way humans do, but they are most definately affected by the death of one of their friends or herd mates.

Depending on their relationship to the horse that passed away.

Horses very often display signs of sadness, even depression at the passing of a friend, family member, or foal.....................**Yes**

How much weight can a horse carry?

Horses are beasts of burden but there is a limit to what they can physically carry without injury.

Researchers have identified a threshold of when a rider is too heavy.

A horse carrying 15 to 20% of its body weight showed little indication of stress.

But when they were packing weights of 25 to 30% their physical signs changed markedly .

The horses had noticeably faster breathing and increased heart rates.

Which horses are reported to be hypoallergenic?

The Bashkir curly horse is claimed to be the only hypoallergenic horse breed. Most people who are allergic to horses can handle being around and owning curly horses without suffering any allergic reactions

Research indicates a protein is missing from the hair of curlies which may my be responsible for allergic reactions to horses from allergy sufferers.

What is Kumis and what has it got to do with horses?

Chances are you have never heard of this mildly alcoholic drink, or had the desire to taste it - especially if you knew it was made from fermented mare's milk. Milking mares is a common practice among the horse people of Mongolia. The milking season typically runs from Mid -June to early October. During one season, a mare produces approximately 1,000 to 1,200 liters of milk of which half is used in the production of Kumis. The other half is left to the foals.

It takes considerable skill to milk a mare:
the milker kneels on one knee, with a pail propped on the other, steadied by a string tied around the arm, with one arm is wrapped behind the mare's hind leg and the other in front. A foal is allowed to suckle to start the milk flow and then is pulled away by another person, but left touching the mare's side during the entire process.

Roses are red, violets are blue
Horses that dont win are made into glue
(a poem an old jockey whispered in the ear of every horse he rode)

Are horses really sent to the glue factory ?

It's mostly used as a figure of speech nowadays. But yes, horses were used in the production of glue.
Rendering plants are the re-cycling links in the food chain. They take everythig no one else can use: bone, cartilage, hooves, dead animals. Most of this animal by product comes from grocery stores and restaraunts.
It is all boiled and ground up and is used in the production of non food products like soap, lubricants, and heavy glue.

Do people eat horse meat?

yes - horse meat is popular in France, Indonesia, Germany, Belgium with China being the largest consumer of horse meat.

What has "Cherry Blossom" got to do with horses?

If you are travelling in Japan and see Cherry blossom meat on the menu, be aware you are ordering horse meat

What is a clothes horse?

Depending on the context, it has two different meanings.
One meaning refers to a laundry accessory, a rack on which to hang wet clothes.

Whilst the other meaning describes someone who is very stylish. A human clothes horse is someone who puts a great deal of energy into dressing fashion-ably. It is used to describe a vain person who invests large amounts of time and money to look good
Both seem to exist solely for the purpose of displaying clothes.

How do horses know when you are scared?
Can they "Smell Fear"

As well as having five highly developed senses horses also have a sixth sense. This is a heightened perception, a quality that is rare in humans. This is not as spooky or mystical as it seems.

You may have heard someone say "I am afraid of this horse and he know it". This is not magic on the horse's part. The horse is acutely aware of the persons body language and posture. He will detect rapid breathing and heightened adrenalin levels, increased sweating due to stress. All signs which clearly tell the horses - this person is fearful.

These small details help him determine if the person is a friend or foe and whether or not he needs to be afraid. A horses intuition picks up a great deal of information from the world around him.

So forget the myth that horses can smell fear - they can pick up fear messages in so many more ways than just smell.

Another Common myth - Are horses are just like dogs?

This is a misconception among those who are not familiar with horses. Sure both animals have been domesticated, but the similarity ends there.

Dogs are carnivores and horses are herbivores.

The dog pack has one leader, the alpha male, and all other members are equal. This a dog still remains faithful, even when owners are cruel to their dog. Man is the Alpha male it is in this dog's nature to be subordinate to him.

On the other hand, horses have a complex hierarchical system, every horse within the herd know his place. Also, If you are cruel to a horse, he will not forget. Don't expect him to be waiting for you at the gate wagging his tail.

Did you know

China not only has the most people in the world, with its vast and varried landscape, China is also home to the most horses in the world with close to 10,000,000 horses and ponies.

Many of the Chinese breeds are small and incredibly hardy; some of them date back well over 3000 years. China is a huge continent. Many breeds are only found in isolated regions, making their blood lines pure.

We hear very little about these breeds. They dont make headlines or get chosen for the Olympic equestrian team. Many are a well kept secret.

It would be fascinating to learn more about China's horses:

Baise horse
Balikun horse
Bose pony
Buohai horse
Chaidamu pony
Datong horse
Debao Pony
Erluchun horse
Guangxi
Guizhou pony
Heihe horse
Hequ
Jielin horse
jinhong horse
Hinzhou horse
Lichuan
Lijiang pony
Sandan horse
Sanhe horse
Sini Horse
Tiger horse
Yanqi horse

Were you born in the year of the Horse?

The Chinese calender uses 12 animals to symbolize each year.

One of those animals is the horse.

For those born in 1906, 1918, 1930, 1942, 1954, 1966, 1978, 1990, 2002, 2014 - the Chinese believe these people have unique characteristics. They are supposedly exciting and extrovert; vivid and animated, the life of any party.

People born in the year of the horse are bursting with energy, they are trustworthy and good confidants.

However, they do like to get their own way and can be a little self centered.

Must a horse with a broken leg must be shot?

One of the common myths surrounding horses that has endured for centuries is that a horse with a broken leg must be put down.

In earlier times, that was most certainly the case.

However modern medical technology has ways to treat such an injury. Surgery can be performed if the fracture is contained to certain small areas; a cast can be applied, or metal implants may be utilized to remedy the issue. Unfortunately, it is very expensive.

How did the Quarter horse get its name?

In the 1600's, early settlers bred the thoroughbred horses they brought with them from England with the native horses owned by the Chickasaw Indians. The resulting horse was small hardy, and fast. He could be worked on the farm during the week and raced on weekends. As flat racing became popular with the colonists, so did this new breed of horse - he could out run the thoroughbreds over a shorter distance (quarter of a mile). There are records of some horses galloping at speeds of 55mph. This is how the Quarter horse got his name. The Quarter horse is the most popular breed of horse in the USA. The American quarter horse registry is the largest in the world with over five million quarter horses registered.

Are horse tranquilizers Deadly to humans?

The basic answer is YES Tranquilizers can even be deadly to horses if they are given the wrong dosage. They work by lowering the body's functions. Depending on the active ingredient (drug) they either lower the heart rate or the depress the nervous system.

Both effects can be deadly for humans.

Is there a hidden meaning behind horse statues?

If you see a statue in the park of a person on a horse, and the horse has both front legs in the air - the person died in battle.

If the horse has one front leg in the air - the person died as a result of the wound he received in battle.

If the horse has all four legs on the ground - the person died of natural causes.

Pony Power

On the island of Hydra in Greece, motorized vehicles are banned. All horse power comes from horses and ponies.

Does the process of branding a horse "Hurt"

Horses have extremely sensitive skin - they can detect when a fly lands on a hair and twitch to shake it off. Their skin is susceptible to sunburn, rain rash, and allergic reactions.

Hot iron branding requires the branding iron to be heated in a fire till it is red hot then held against the horses skin until the mark is burnt into his hide. The underlying skin is so damaged that hairs in that area do not grow back, Creating a permanent identification mark.

Freeze branding - uses a similar branding iron, however this time it is frozen using liquid nitrogen - it is held against the horse's side long enough to kill the cells in the horses skin that produce pigmentation, but not too long because that would create a big blister. Freeze branding Results in a white brand. It is common practice, to sedate horses before freeze branding.

Why do horses stampede?

Does it hurt?   You decide.

We have all seen the dramatic horse stampedes played out in the old fashioned western movies. They are usually started by the firing of guns.

These stampedes were staged and hopefully carried out in a safe way. Anything unusual may start a stampede, especially at night when everything is still and quiet, and possible dangers lurk in the dark.

Sudden loud noises, a lightening strike, wild animals spooking the herd.

Once the herd takes flight, fear and adrenaline takes hold and they move as one thundering mass, destroying anything in their path.

The notion that a galloping horse will try to avoid trampling a human does not apply when a herd of horses are stampeding.

Magnetic Therapy - fact or fiction?

Magnetic therapy has long been believed to relieve pain and promote natural healing. Magnets were used by the ancient Egyptians and Greeks. The writings of Aristotle mentioned magnets in healing, they have been used in Chinese medicine from around 2000 BC.

Today it is claimed that magnetic therapy is a safe and effective method of relieving pain and promoting health on both humans and animals including horses. Like any alternative healing method (that hasn't been scientifically proven) there are those who swear by it, and there are also skeptics.

What about Horses in History?

From the ice age to the industrial age horses have shaped civilisations across the world. In this final chapter, I have gathered a few snippets from history that will enlighten and entertain you.

Medieval Horse breeds (England)

In the Dark Ages, horses were used for transportation, farming and warfare. The most valued horses were **Destiers** these favored by Noblemen and knights because they were taller and of a solid color. They were the "war horses".
Palfrey's were the everyday horse of a knight. This breed was shorter than the Destier, Noblewomen would also ride the Palfrey because of its smooth gait.
The Courser was the fastest horse of the middle ages, and was used as a messenger horse. It was also favored by kings because of its speed.
The Rouncy horses were work horses of the day and were used on farms. They were the horse of the lower class.

The Pony Express - was only in operation for 19 months

Founded by William H.Russell, William b. Waddell and Alexander Majors
The pony express consisted of relays of riders carrying saddlebags of mail across a 2000 mile trail. The service officially opened on April 3, 1860. Pony riders covered 250 miles in a 24 hour day.
At its peak, the pony express had more than 100 stations, 80 riders and between 400 - 500 horses. The express route was extremely hazardous, yet only one mail delivery was ever lost. The Pacific telegraph line was completed in 1861 which ended the need for the Pony express.

Traffic Pollution is nothing new

You may think there are a lot of yellow cabs in New York today. Did you know that in the early 1900's, around 130,000 horses worked in Manhattan (more than ten times the amount of yellow cabs today).
It would have been a dirty smelly place - Horses produce up to 45 lbs of manure and 7.5 liters of urine every day.

Motorized horse power

Some of the technical pioneers in the US had a great appreciation for horses in fact some cars were named after them:

Ford Bronco 1966 - 1996   Dodge Colt 1970 - 1994
Ford Pinto 1971 - 1980   Ford Mustang 1964 - present

In the beginning

Species of equus have been around for more than five million years.

Horses were first domesticated about 3000 years ago.
They were first controlled by a rope around the lower jaw, a primitive hackamore or a ring through the nose like oxen.

The first metal bits

originated in the Near East around 1500 BC. Both straight and jointed mouthpieces with ornate cheek-pieces appeared at the same time. These often very severe bits were worn by the chariot horses.

Curb bits appeared around the 4th Century BC and were worn by medieval war horses.

Who designed the first saddle?

Saddles first appeared in history over 4,000 years ago, but the earliest designs were little more than a patch of animal hide tied on the horse to soften the ride. This idea caught on and the hide cloths became more elaborate and were attached by girths. There are records of Assyrian warriors riding atop decorative saddle cloths around 700 BC.
Moving North towards Siberia the Scythians created saddlery that was beautiful and functional. A frozen tomb from the 5th century BC contained an ornately decorated saddle made from leather, felt, hair, and gold.

But it wasn't until 200 BC that horsemen started to be concerned for the horses well being and designed a wooden framed padded saddle that kept the riders weight off the horse's vertebrae.

Mounted Police

Police horses have been used in peace time law enforcement since the 17th century. The first official mounted police unit was established in 1805 in London, England. The unit was a huge success and in a few years, both Australia and America had adopted the idea.
The Royal Canadian Mounted Police was founded in May 1873.

Who took care of sick horses?

For as long as there have been horses, there have been "experts" and healers. Many of their cures and practices now seem extremely bizarre.

In the 17th century, it was believed that if you drew blood from a horse then got him to drink his own blood this would cure all kinds of equine ailments including worms.

In 1762 the first veterinary college designed to train horse healers was founded in Lyon France by Claude Bourgelat. He was a leading authority on horse management.

In 1891, the first edition of the book "Veterinary country practice" was published. This book was targeted towards Chemists. Within the pages were 11 different recipes for Horse de-wormers, using ingredients such as Aloes, ginger, garlic, Valerian, liquorice even small amounts of arsenic.

Poisons were popular

Chemical wormers were introduced in 1940, but those early chemicals like phenothiazine were very toxic and didn't kill all types of parasites.

By the 1950s, vets had realized that by mixing small amounts of different chemicals their concoction would attack more varieties of worms. But they had to be administered by a vet using a tube down the horses throat, (a drench) this process that also carried risks.

Modern Methods

It wasn't until the 1970s that horse owners could de-worm their own horses without having to call the vet.

New drugs and chemicals are continually being developed as the war on equine parasites wages on. Parasites are persistent and because they learn to adapt to their environments, they develop a resistance to the drugs over time.

The manufacturers of De-wormers readily promote how good they are at killing off unwanted parasites.

However, very little is said about what possible side effects stronger drugs and chemicals will have on the horse.

What is a "Hipposandal"?

Hoof health and wear and tear has always been a priority with horsemen. During the first century the Romans made shoes for their horses from leather and metal called Hipposandals. The boot-like device consisted of a metal sole that curled up around the hoof to encase it. It was held in place with leather straps.

By the 6th century European horsemen had begun nailing metal shoes to their horses. These early horse shoes were made of cast bronze.

It took another few hundred years before iron horse shoes were widely used all across Europe.

It wasn't until the 16th century that the process of heating a horse shoe, and shaping it to fit the hoof before nailing it onto the horse became the norm. Blacksmiths would pre make shoes in a variety of sizes, then adjust them to fit, as they were needed.

The Horseshoe revolution

In 1835, the first U.S. patent for a horseshoe manufacturing machine was issued to Henry Burden of Troy New York - his machine would make 60 horseshoes per hour.

Who invented "Horse cubes"?

Spiller's created the original compound horse food in the 1950s. Other feed manufacturer soon followed their lead in providing a balanced mixture of horse feed in a convenient cube form.

Did you know; There are 188 verses in the Bible that mention horses, all the way from Genesis to Revelations. My favorite verse is;

"I saw heaven opened and behold, a white horse, and He who sat on it is called faithful and true" *Revelations 9:11*

This reassures me that there are horses in heaven.

What is the "Sport of Kings"?

Horse racing has been around since 4500 BC. Its origins began with the prehistoric tribesmen of central Asia, who first domesticated horses.

In 638 BC, horse racing and chariot racing were featured in the Greek Olympics. The sport became a public obsession within the Roman empire. Modern racing began in England, in the 12th century, when knights returning from the crusades with swift Arabian horses would race against each other in two horse races. Placing large wagers on the two horse races became a popular pastime of nobility which is how it got its name "Sport of Kings".

More Arabian stallions were imported and bred with English mares to produce horses that combined speed with endurance, creating the Thoroughbred.

The earliest records of horses racing in England date back to 1530 in York. The first race course was opened in Chester in 1540.

British settlers brought horse racing to the New World - America. The first race track was laid in Long Island in 1665. Over the next couple of hundred years, race tracks popped up around the New York area. They were operated by the rich and famous to showcase their horses.

In 1791, the Jockey Club was formed to establish a "general stud book" and rules for racing. Only Thoroughbreds were allowed to race, horses that could trace their blood lines to the founding stallions, the Byerley Turk, Darley Arabian and the Godolphin Arabian

Today horse racing is just as popular. Of course its accessible to everyone, not just kings, but owning, and training a race horse still requires lots of money.

Final Though

If you have ever owned or ridden horses, you will have an appreciation for how much they want to please us. They try their best to help us achieve our goals no matter what discipline as humans we pursue.

They go faster when pushed – jump higher when asked - try difficult dressage moves, even overcome their own natural fears in order to be obedient and to please.

They choose to have a relationship with us.

My final question – to which I really don't know the answer, is
WHY?

Ode to the Horse
Where in this wide world can man find nobility without pride,
Friendship without envy
Or beauty without vanity?
Here, where grace is laced with muscle, and strength by gentleness confined.
He serves without servility; he has fought without enmity.
There is nothing so powerful, nothing less violent, there is nothing so quick,
nothing more patient.
England's past has been borne on his back.
All our history is his industry; we are his heirs, he our inheritance.
The Horse!
By Ronald Duncan
written in 1954

The Horse Watcher

Linda Finstad

Your mission should you choose to accept it is to become a "Horse Watcher"

Horse watchers are on their own spiritual journey.
There is no prize or ribbon for being the best
No certificate to say you have learn all there is to learn.
No 100% right or wrong answers
In fact just as you discover the answer to one question - 10 more take its place.
But it requires no special equipment or physical prowess
Whether you are 8 or 80 years old, there is always something new to discover

Horse watching won't make you richer, fitter or more beautiful, but it will feed
your soul, calm your spirit and develop your appreciation for nature.

For more information visit
www.thehorsewatcher.com

Research acknowledgments and Citations

Zrotsos RVY, P., & Santschi DVM, E. (1998). Stalking the Lethal White Syndrome. Paint Horse Journal, (July 1998), 1-1. Retrieved from http://ads.apha.com/Sitefinity_Website_Images/breed/lethalwhites03.html

The Straight Dope Science Advisory Board. (2000). Are horses really made into glue? The Straight Dope, 1. Retrieved from http://www.straightdope.com/columns/read/1860/are-horses-really-made-into-glue

Horse breeds from China. (2011, August 1). Retrieved from http://www.theequinest.com/breeds-china/

http://www.equisearch.com/article/eqsaddleev619

Sellnow, L. (1999, January 1). Fetal development and foal growth. Retrieved from http://www.thehorse.com/articles/10257/fetal-development-and-foal-growth

Smith BVS, A. (2006, January 1). Normal signs of behavior before and including foaling in mares. Retrieved from http://horsetalk.co.nz/2012/10/17/foaling-in-mares/

Barteau, Y. (2007, September 1). Understanding Horse Personalities, Part 1: The 4 Basic Personality Types - See more at: Http://dressagetoday.com/article/horse_personalities_basic_types_030509#sthash.MMzLfogo.dpuf. Retrieved from http://dressagetoday.com/article/horse_personalities_basic_types_030509

Foal rejection. (n.d.). Retrieved from http://www.usask.ca/wcvm/herdmed/applied-ethology/behaviourproblems/foalreject.html

Heusner, G. (1993). Horse Breeding. Retrieved from http://www.dancinghorse.net/ranch/breeding.html

Sutor, C. (1999, June 1). WHat is your horse saying. Retrieved from http://www.equusite.com/articles/behavior/behaviorSounds.shtml

Polny, E., & Denis, M. (2010, February 1). What does it mean when horses yawn. Retrieved from http://www.training-horses-naturally.com/what-does-it-mean-when-horses-yawn.html

Schonholtz, C. (2012, January 1). Professional rodeo horses are bred to buck. Retrieved from http://www.naiaonline.org/naia-library/articles/professional-rodeo-horses-are-bred-to-buck/

Sellnow, L. (1998). Foal Imprinting. The Horse Your Guide to Equine Health. Retrieved from http://www.thehorse.com/articles/10405/foal-imprinting

Cable, DVM, C. (2001). Foal rejection. Retrieved from http://www.thehorse.com/articles/10702/foal-rejection

Equine Self mutilation. (n.d.). Retrieved from http://www.usask.ca/wcvm/herdmed/applied-ethology/behaviourproblems/eqselfmutilate.html

How does a horse learn. (n.d.). Retrieved from http://www.equiworld.net/uk/training/horse/pschology.htm

Blocksdorf, K. (n.d.). Understanding how your horse sees. Retrieved from http://horses.about.com/od/understandinghorses/a/Understanding-How-Your-Horse-Sees.htm

Smith Thomas, H. (2007). Moon Blindness. Retrieved from http://www.thehorse.com/articles/18087/moon-blindness

Types of Equine colic. (n.d.). Retrieved from http://www.coliccrusade.com/what-is-equine-colic/types-of-equine-colic/

What is Laminitis. (n.d.). Retrieved from http://www.animedvets.co.uk/laminitis.htm
Sellnow, L. (2013). What's a splint. Retrieved from http://www.thehorse.com/articles/12422/whats-a-splint

Prescott, D. (2003, April 1). Strangles in horses. Retrieved from http://www.omafra.gov.on.ca/english/livestock/horses/facts/03-037.htm

Blocksdorf, K. (n.d.). Quidding. Retrieved rom http://horses.about.com/od/DentitionanDigestion/fl/Quidding-When-A-Horse-Spits-Out-Wet-Bundles-of-Hay.htm

Other animals. (n.d.). A Complete Guide to the Types of Worms Affecting Horses and the Drugs Effective Against Them. Retrieved from http://www.medicanimal.com/Other-Animals/Horse/Horse/Supplements-and-Wormers/Wormers/A-Complete-Guide-to-the-Types-of-Worms-Affecting-Horses-and-the-Drugs-Effective-Against-them/a/ART111545

Foster, & Smith. (n.d.). Troublesome ticks. Ticks on Horses: How to Identify Anf Control. Retrieved from http://www.drsfostersmith.com/pic/article.cfm?aid=1814

Przewalski's Horse. (n.d.). Retrieved from http://animals.nationalgeographic.com/animals/mammals/przewalskis-horse/

Frank, K. (n.d.). Living with locoweed. Western Horseman.

What are horse chestnuts and ergots. (n.d.). Retrieved from http://www.cowboyway.com/What/WhatAreChestnuts.htm
Rider, S. (2011, October 1). Retrieved from http://www.snarkyrider.com/2011/10/06/the-tale-of-a-draft-horse/
How many breeds of horses are there. (n.d.). Retrieved from http://www.webertrainingstables.com/breed-numbers

Breeds of donkey. (n.d.). Retrieved from http://www.theequinest.com/donkey-breeds/

Skelly, C., & Griffin, A. (2011, February 1). Natural and artificial gaits of the horse. Retrieved from http://myhorseuniversity.com/resources/eTips/April_2011/Didyouknow

Lamie, R. (2010, July 1). Retrieved from http://www.neatorama.com/2010/07/15/12-essential-facts-about-the-folks-who-race-horses/

History of Dressage. (n.d.). Retrieved from http://www.equine-world.co.uk/horse_sports/history_dressage.asp

Liyou, D. (2005, July 1). Wolf teeth in horses. Retrieved from http://evds.net.au/article_wolf_teeth.php

History of Dressage. (n.d.). Retrieved from http://www.equine-world.co.uk/horse_sports/history_dressage.asp

Liyou, D. (2005, July 1). Wolf teeth in horses. Retrieved from http://evds.net.au/article_wolf_teeth.php

The fine art photography by Linda Finstad
featured in this book
is available as
Limited edition Giclee fine art prints
Signed / numbered with a certificate of authenticity limited to 250 prints

Linda loves to share her wit and wisdom with other horse lovers;

She offers the **"How to think like a horse"** workshop

That can be used as a fundraiser for
Pony club, 4H, Riding schools, Equine retreats, Animal rescue facilities
Agricultural Societies, Colleges, tack stores etc.

for details please visit
www.TheHorseWatcher.com

Made in the USA
Charleston, SC
28 March 2015